REV. FRANCIS R. DAVIS
ST. PATRICK'S CHURCH
274 DENISON PKWY. E.
CORNING, NEW YORK 14830-2995

# LITURGY—OUR SCHOOL OF FAITH

# LITURGY—OUR SCHOOL OF FAITH

by

Anthony M. Buono

ALBA · HOUSE  NEW · YORK

SOCIETY OF ST. PAUL, 2187 VICTORY BLVD., STATEN ISLAND, NEW YORK 10314

*Library of Congress Cataloging in Publication Data*

Buono, Anthony M.
  Liturgy, our school of faith.

  1. Catholic Church—Liturgy. 2. Catholic
Church—Education. 3. Spiritual life—Catholic
authors. 4. Christian education. I. Title.
BX1970.B78     1982     264'.02     82-16328
ISBN 0-8189-0435-6

Nihil Obstat:
William B. Smith, S.T.D.
Censor Librorum

Imprimatur:
†Joseph T. O'Keefe, D.D.
Vicar General
Archdiocese of New York
October 2, 1982

The Nihil Obstat and Imprimatur are
a declaration that a book or pamphlet is considered
to be free from doctrinal or moral error. It it is not implied
that those who have granted the Nihil Obstat and
Imprimatur agree with the contents,
opinions or statements expressed.

---

Designed, printed and bound in the United States of
America by the Fathers and Brothers of the
Society of St. Paul, 2187 Victory Boulevard,
Staten Island, New York 10314, as part of their
communications apostolate.

---

1 2 3 4 5 6 7 8 9 (Current Printing: first digit)

---

© Copyright 1982 by the Society of St. Paul

## CONTENTS

Preface ....................................................... VII
1. The Eucharist and Daily Life ................................. 3
2. The Role of the Liturgical Assembly ......................... 11
3. Bible and Liturgy: Christ's Presence in the Word ............ 23
4. The Eucharist: Sacrifice, Memorial, and Presence ............ 35
5. Whatever Happened to the Commentator? ....................... 43
6. Liturgy and Creativity ...................................... 51
7. Liturgical Spirituality ..................................... 57
8. The Role of Silence in Liturgical Celebrations .............. 65
9. The Need for Liturgical Catechesis .......................... 71
10. Liturgical Adaptation: Celebration of Major American Holidays ... 81
11. Christ in the Liturgy: The Expectation of the Nations ...... 91
12. The Holy Spirit: The Soul of the Liturgy ................... 97
13. Mary in the Liturgy: A Sure Guide to True Marian Devotion ... 107
14. The Liturgical Celebration of the Saints ................... 121
15. The Sacraments and Sacramentals: Christifying the Universe ... 131
16. The Liturgy of the Hours: The Sanctification of Time ....... 143
17. Liturgical and Non-Liturgical Prayer: Praying with the Church ... 155
18. A "Liturgical Person"—A Person Who Loves Life .............. 167
Footnotes .................................................... 175

# ACKNOWLEDGMENTS

Chapter 3 incorporates some material that originally appeared in the *Eucharist* magazine, published by the Society of the Blessed Sacrament, New York, N.Y.

Chapters 5, 6, and 7 originally appeared as articles in *Pastoral Life* magazine, published by the Society of St. Paul, Canfield, Ohio.

The author and publisher are grateful to these publishers for permission to use the above material.

The brief quotations of Mass texts are taken from the *Sacramentary* copyrighted 1974 by the International Committee on English in the Liturgy. Used with permission.

# PREFACE

"Do you love money?" the Bible sales manager asked me.
I murmured, "I could sure use it," startled by this question.
The crisp retort came quickly. "I didn't ask if you could use it, I asked if you loved it."
As I look back now, I realize this observer of sales personnel had guessed that I wouldn't be good at selling on commission. Indeed he was correct for I worked for all of one day and didn't even sell a single Bible.
I was thrilled at the idea of opening the doors of the Holy Bible to many people but selling them was quite a different matter. I didn't love money!
Most Catholics show the same attitude toward the Liturgy that I had toward money. They like it but not too much. They know they can use its help but they do not have a love for it. Yet without this love they cannot make the Liturgy a real part of their lives. Without this love, they will live in two different worlds—their Christianity on Sunday and their ordinary lives the rest of the week.
Liturgy is, after all, the *action part* of prayer. It is *prayer in action*, the *Bible in action*, a dialogue between God and His people. Ideally, it should take hold of us and imbue us with God's life, God's thoughts and God's plan. These God-like attitudes should then permeate our ordinary activities on a daily basis. We can then live more fully in a kind of sacramentalized world—Christianizing everyone and everything we encounter on our day-to-day earthly pilgrimage.
This is a sublime ideal that is all too seldom attained but it can be approached. Liturgy can be applied to our lives—if only we learn how to do it. The aim and purpose of this book is to explain some specific ways in which this can be done. In this respect it is a book concerning pastoral Liturgy.
At the same time the information is based on the solid studies of liturgiologists. Consequently, it is in full accord with the genuine teaching of the Church on the Liturgy.

In a sense, we can accommodate to Liturgy the aphorism applied to Christianity: "It is not that the Liturgy has been tried and found wanting but that the Liturgy has never really been tried at all!"

The present book asks everyone to try the Liturgy. When rightly understood and carried out with full participation, the Liturgy of the Church will become the summit of life's activities.

# LITURGY—OUR SCHOOL OF FAITH

by

Anthony M. Buono

Chapter 1
# THE EUCHARIST AND DAILY LIFE

The decrees of the Second Vatican Council, the reforms of the Liturgy, and the documents of the last few Popes have spelled out the fact that the Liturgy places us in contact with the Risen Christ—through Whom and for Whom all things have been created. This is especially true of the Eucharistic Liturgy, which is the Sacrament to which all others are related. The Eucharist is the visible and effective mode of Christ's invisible and transfigured presence in the universe.

As of now it is all too evident that for many this primacy of the Eucharist is nonexistent. It plays little part in their "real" lives. The Eucharist remains for them simply a kind of object whose validity rests entirely in itself, and absorbs religious activity instead of making it work as a leaven in their lives for the salvation of everything in the universe. It is kept in an artificial world of ritualism which is completely cut off from the true reality of their lives.

If we were to question Christians streaming out of churches after a celebration of the Eucharist, we would very likely receive textbook answers about the Eucharist but encounter little real understanding of the role it must play in everyday life.

Those queried would show little knowledge of how to integrate the Eucharist into their lives, and even less understanding of how those lives should revolve around the Eucharist.

Perhaps most unfortunate of all, such Christians would regard the Eucharist as something that remains in Church and is set apart from their ordinary activities—which are inferior to any religious actions. At the same time, such Christians do not want to give up their ordinary lives for Liturgy. Thus they live a kind of schizoid existence—believing that they are not really doing what God wants them to do.

They think God wants them to be religious—but they do not realize that they are lay people who have a spirituality of their own. The Eucharist is a large part of that spirituality—only not in the way they think!

One reason for this lack of understanding is that we hear very little about how the Liturgy influences our lives. We must make a conscious effort to see that the Eucharist extends to every phase of the universe. We must apply our ingenuity to bring it to every circumstance in some way.

A powerful example of such total liturgical awareness was unwittingly provided by a woman at an evening weekday Eucharist some years ago. Just before the start of the service, a jetliner had crashed on a highway outside Kennedy Airport in New York. At the Prayer of the Faithful, when petitions were being voiced, she added: "For the victims of the plane that has just crashed, let us pray to the Lord."

Those few words took our local Eucharist with our self-centered concerns and transformed it into what it really is—a world-saving and universal-centered event. It brought home to all those present that we were engaged in the most important event of our lives for the good of the world. At that very moment our Eucharist was Christianizing the world, and specifically in this case, the tragic crash that had just occurred. It was infusing that catastrophe with grace [Christ's energy], and transforming it, bringing it into line with the thrust of the world that is advancing toward the Plenitude of Christ.

Our Eucharist was giving life to the dead and grace to the living who were in any way touched by this evil. Inevitably, as only God's grace can, it would bring good out of that evil in countless unforeseen and hidden ways.

### Christifying the Universe

We are in desperate need of this kind of awareness today. Many regard the Eucharist as an almost banal event, divested of its mystery by the deceptive idea that "we know everything that is going on" because the whole rite is in the vernacular. We must realize that such an attitude is exactly the opposite of the reality.

To obtain a true idea of the role of the Eucharist in our lives we must see the world with the eyes of the Bible. We will then see that humanity is the chosen instrument of our Redemption. Christ came to endure pain, to suffer and die in the flesh; and He *rose* in the flesh. Hence, flesh and inanimate matter are associated with the Savior's mission and His victory over death.

We can make use of all the resources of the universe in working out our salvation. In the words of the Roman Canon of the Mass (Eucharistic Prayer I): "Through Christ our Lord You give us all these gifts. You fill them with life and goodness, You bless them and make them holy."

We must realize—as the Bible continually shows us—that people master the cosmos and by their daily work make perfect the divine image in them. Through their work and social relationships they attain a community of interpersonalism based on love, and they reach God through love of neighbor. As individuals and as members of a community, they open their whole beings to the worship of God, their Creator.

In the final analysis one single operation is taking place through all the events and vicissitudes of life in this world of individuals—the annexation of Christ to His chosen ones through His Mystical Body. This entire process is dependent on our freedom as well as on God's grace. The growth of the world falls under the influence of Christ through the free cooperation of human beings.

It is the task of Christ's Church to Christify the universe. By the Resurrection, the Body of Christ became coextensive with the universe to which it had been organically bound by the Incarnation. But individual incorporation into this Body becomes a reality only through the Church and the Eucharist.

When Christ descends sacramentally into each of His faithful, it is not only to commune with that person. When, through the priest, He says: "This is My Body," those words go beyond the fragment of bread over which they are said. They give birth to the whole Mystical Body. In this way, the Eucharist reaches out to the whole world and brings Christ's saving grace to it.

In a sense the true substance to be offered and transformed in the Eucharist is the world's development during each day. The bread symbolizes what creation succeeds in producing. The wine (blood) symbolizes what creation causes to be lost in exhaustion and suffering in the course of its effort.

Thus the transubstantiation of bread and wine into the Eucharistic Body and Blood of Jesus is extended into the evolving world including the totality of all the joys and pains that result from the divinely ordained developing process. Christ gathers up all these joys and sufferings and offers them to the Father. He causes them to become salvific for all who experience them.

It follows that the Eucharist is not only the Sacrament which consecrates the bread and wine into the "Physical" Body of Christ. It is also the Sacrament which consecrates the human community into His Mystical

Body. In this way the Sacrifice of Christ is also actualized and accomplished in the community, so that this community becomes a community offering itself to God in virtue of its unity with the Sacrifice of Jesus.

As a result we can say in a broad fashion that the Eucharist includes a true consecration of humankind. The entire world is offered and transformed by Christ's saving grace through the mediation of the Church in the Eucharist. Or put another way, the saving merits won by Christ through His passion and Resurrection are applied to the world and everything in it here and now.

This consecration of humankind and the world takes place in a sacramental manner—which is therefore imperfect and calls for completion. Christ has accomplished this definitive act of offering. But for the Christian community and for the Church, the sacrifice will not be fully accomplished until the end of time.

The Eucharist is both the announcement and the anticipation of the transformation of the cosmos. At each Mass, symbolized by the oblations, the entire Church—the soul of the world, as it were—offers herself to be consecrated to God by sharing in the death and resurrection of Jesus. She celebrates anew the Passover, the passage of Christ from His earthly state to His glorified state.

The sacramental words of consecration fall directly on the bread and the wine, but the transubstantiation is encircled by a halo of divinization—real though less intense—that extends to the whole universe.

The Eucharist in space and time perpetually builds up the Church. Moreover, in virtue of the connections of the human being with the universe, the extensions of the Eucharist little by little reach all elements of the cosmos.

In the totality of its operation, the Eucharist is nothing less than the expression and manifestation of God's unifying energy applied to each spiritual atom of the universe. To adhere to Christ is inevitably to incorporate ourselves a little more on each occasion in a "Christogenesis," the upbuilding of the Body of Christ. This goes hand in hand with the upbuilding of the universe according to God's plan.

The universe is gradually subjected to the transforming activities of Christ living in us through the life He brings us in the Blessed Sacrament. Through our loving submission to Him, His life is extended to the subhuman cosmos. His Sacred Humanity takes on a particular area of the world to transform it into a united Eucharistic hymn of praise to the Eternal Father.

## Full Meaning of Sacramental Reception

We could say that the whole life of Christians—both on earth and in heaven—is a kind of perpetual Eucharistic union. The Divine comes to us only as "informed" by Christ. This is the principal law of our supernatural life.

God's general presence is constantly backed by a particular presence of Christ according to His resurrected human nature. This presence of Christ grows in proportion to the state of grace in us. It is capable not only of enduring but also of being intensified by the whole miscellaneous corpus of what we do and what we suffer.

It is literally true that whatever Christians do, it is done unto Christ. This justifies us in our belief that we can in strict fact live always and everywhere without being separated from Christ. To love one's brothers and sisters and to receive the Body of Christ is not simply to obey and merit a reward; it is organically to build up, element by element, the living unity of the Plenitude of Christ—the Body of Christ.

Thus, grace does more than attach us by its spiritual instillation to the divinity of the Word. It brings with it a certain progressive inclusion in a created organism which is physically centered on the resurrected Humanity of Christ.

This "habitual" Communion effected by sanctifying grace between Christ and the faithful gives its full meaning to sacramental reception of the Sacred Species. The latter is simply the tightening—especially chosen and wonderfully active—of a looser union established and maintained by the state of grace.

Long before any individual Communion was received, a first and permanent connection through the operation of Baptism is formed between the Christian and the Body of Christ. And after each Communion, in spite of the disappearance of the Sacred Species, which had for a time raised it to a special degree of intimacy and importance, this connection persists—more strongly established even though in a less concentrated form.

Therefore, sacramental Communion ceases to be a discontinuous element in a Christian's life and becomes the fabric from which it is woven. It is the accentuation and the renewal of a permanent state which attaches us continuously to Christ.

The new Liturgy restored to the sacramental rites of the Church the overshadowed concept that everyone has a definite task to carry out in those rites. Just as each one of us has a task to perform in life, so in our Liturgical Celebrations each of us also has a task to carry out, and as is true in our lives, if we do not carry out that task no one else will.

The Church has stressed that the role of the people is just as necessary as—though objectively less important than—the role of the celebrant and ministers. For the Eucharistic Celebration is an action of the community assembled together to render worship to God. This requires both external and internal participation on the part of all present.

One type of participation alone is not sufficient. We cannot be present at the celebration merely with a kind of "devout attendance," relying on the people on the altar to do all the work. We must also do our part. We must enlist not only our minds and our hearts in the service of God's worship but our bodies as well: our tongues and lips, our hands and feet, our arms and legs, etc. For it is the whole person who is called to praise and glorify the Creator.

This does not mean that we must be totally preoccupied with external responses to every word or action of the celebrant and ministers. But it does mean that we must make a concerted effort to respond whenever we can do so without turning that response into a mere formality devoid of any interior attitude behind it. By dwelling on the content of our parts, we can participate at every Mass fully, actively and consciously in accord with the fervent desire of the Church.[1]

This participation is a right and a duty of the Laity that had been shunted aside over the years. It arises by reason of our Baptism which makes us a chosen race, a royal priesthood.[2] Thus, in the Church all are ministers though in different degrees and with diverse roles and offices, and worship is carried out by all—as the act of all and for all.

We should participate at every Eucharist as *co-celebrants* (not non-celebrants, however) with the celebrant and ministers. We come to be instructed with God's Word and nourished at the table of the Lord's Body. We give thanks to God and we offer the Immaculate Victim not only through the hands of the celebrant but *with him*, and in so doing we also offer ourselves.

If we do this, we will unfailingly be drawn day by day into ever more perfect union with God and with one another, so that finally God will be all in all.[3]

**Living the Eucharist**

The Sunday Eucharist that brings together the local Church of which they form a part is the major Liturgy in the lives of the ordinary faithful. It consecrates the particular joys and sorrows of their community as well as those of the whole world. By replenishing themselves at this source weekly, Catholics remain in touch with Christ and live a completely Christian spirituality in the world.

The key point in all this is to make sure that all of us advance the progress of the world during the rest of the week. To do so means to commune with the Eucharist at its source and carry forward its power to transform all things in Christ. Thus, the Eucharist is for us the power station of the Church, enabling us to achieve the Body of Christ through the progress of the world in whatever area we work.

Some of the detailed aspects of this human progress that flow from the Eucharist have been delineated by Pope John Paul II:

> It is from the Eucharist that all of us receive the grace and strength for daily living—to live real Christian lives, in the joy of knowing that God loves us, that Christ died for us, and that the Holy Spirit lives in us.
>
> Our full participation in the Eucharist is the real source of the Christian spirit that we wish to see in our personal lives and in all aspects of society. Whether we serve in politics, in the economic, cultural, social, or scientific field—no matter what our occupation is—the Eucharist is a challenge to our daily lives. . . .
>
> Our union with Christ in the Eucharist must be expressed in the truth of our lives today—in our actions, in our behavior, in our life style, and in our relationships with others. For each one of us the Eucharist is a call to ever greater effort, so that we may live as true followers of Jesus: truthful in our speech, generous in our deeds, concerned, respectful of the dignity and rights of all persons, whatever their rank or income, self-sacrificing, fair and just, kind, considerate, compassionate and self-controlled—looking to the well-being of our families, our young people, our country, Europe and the world.
>
> The truth of our union with Jesus Christ in the Eucharist is tested by whether or not we really love our fellow men and women; it is tested by how we treat others; especially our families: husbands and wives, children and parents, brothers and sisters. It is tested by whether or not we try to be reconciled with our enemies, on whether or not we forgive those who hurt us or offend us. It is tested by whether we practice in life what our faith teaches us.[4]

again, because of changed circumstances since the 5th century when this text was introduced into the rite, the psalm has been dropped and only the antiphon remains. This text gives the particular nuance for the reception of Communion for each day. It allows us to vary our reflections for receiving Christ from day to day in accord with the Liturgical Year.

In Masses with singing this text gives way to a Communion hymn which has the same purpose. It enables us to unite ourselves with Jesus and also with one another in the assembly.

After Communion the celebrant performs the ablutions and a period of silence follows—for personal or public thanksgiving. Then the concluding Prayer after Communion is said by the celebrant in the name of all. It sums up the sentiments of the people, inspired by the Communion antiphon, and we show this by our assent: Amen.

Finally, the celebrant blesses the assembly in the name of the Trinity and sends the members forth to bring Christ into their daily lives and relationships. The people answer with a last word of assent: "Thanks be to God," and then sing a Recessional hymn, officially closing the celebration in a customary way.

This brief review shows the pivotal place that the People's Parts hold in the Eucharist. A conscientious attempt to carry out the parts with understanding and fervor will lead inevitably to greater knowledge, deeper love, and fuller living of the Mass in our lives.

Chapter 2
# THE ROLE OF THE LITURGICAL ASSEMBLY

On any given Sunday a group of persons come together to perform the sacred actions of Christian worship in a particular place. At first, they are barely aware of one another; then they begin to act in unison: they rise, sing, perform actions, pray, and utter responses. They welcome the presiding member of the assembly (the priest who acts in the person of Christ) as indispensable for what they are doing, they listen to him, and they give their assent to the prayer that he makes in the name of all.

This is the Christian assembly. It is rooted in the profoundly human reality of "togetherness" and in the words of Christ: "Where two or three are gathered in My Name, I am in their midst" (Mt 18:20). All religions have some kind of reunions for worship. Christianity alone, however, transforms the simple reunion into an assembly, a sign of the reunion that the God of revelation brings about throughout the History of Salvation.

One of the most misunderstood and unappreciated symbols of our Christian worship is precisely the symbol of this assembly and its liturgical role. Perhaps the overriding reason for this is that there is nothing quite like it in daily life.

One liturgist has stated, the assembly "is not a town meeting, not a neighborhood council, not an elite, not a gathering of cronies, not a party for friends, not a household event, not tribal, not family, not civic, not ideological, not an occasion for manifesting ecclesiastical distinctions."[5]

The assembly is the overwhelming manifestation and realization-in-action of the unity of the Body of Christ, the oneness of the baptized. It is the covenant-celebration of the mission entrusted by God to His people to Christianize the world, to bring to it the Good News of Salvation and endow it with the freedom and the oneness of Christ.

Hence, the Liturgy is ultimately more than just objects or things. The Liturgy which flows from the assembly is a series of prayerful and self-sustaining actions of a faith-community. Members of the assembly are more than simply consumers, clients, or patients. They are the Church which is the fundamental doer, actor and minister of the Liturgy.

Out of the assembly come the priest who presides, the deacon who ministers to him, the acolytes who assist him, the lectors who proclaim God's Word, the extraordinary ministers who administer Christ's Body and Blood (to those physically present as well as to those who make up its extension because of inability to be present), the choristers who create the mood of the celebration, the ushers who insure the good physical order of the celebration, and various others.

### The Assembly in Scripture

In the Old dispensation, it was always God who gathered His people in assembly. He assembled His chosen people in the desert by calling them out of Egyptian bondage (Dt 4:10). The initiative came from God through His spokesperson (Ex 19:4). It was the call of God that created the assembly—not membership in a certain social, cultural, or political stratum, nor the simple sharing of like sentiments, nor even the desire to celebrate an act of worship together.

On reaching Sinai, the people gathered at the foot of the mountain (Ex 19:17). There they listened to the Word of the Covenant which set forth God's plan to make them a "holy nation." In order that the Word proclaimed might be not only understood but also truly constitutive and make them a people, Moses commented on it. The assembly showed its faith by uttering *"Amen"* and by uniting with the ritual act of sacrifice carried out by Moses in their name: "the blood of the Covenant" (Ex 24:8).

At the same time, the assembly's profession of faith was rendered interior by an act of thanksgiving for God's wonders which accompanied the act of worship.

After Sinai, God continued to call His people to assembly. After the people crossed the Jordan and entered the Holy Land under Joshua, they came together in assembly (Jos 24). Joshua proclaimed the wondrous works accomplished by God and obtained a confirmation from the assembly of their faith in God. Then the Covenant was sealed by the act of erecting an altar to God.

After the Babylonian Exile, the remnant was brought in assembly under Ezra the Scribe (Ne 8, 9). Once again God encountered His people in a liturgical action and a festive program. All listened to the reading of God's Word to them *that day*, gave their solemn approval by uttering their Amen, and acknowledged their sins. The lengthy thanksgiving for God's saving deeds concluded with a joyous meal.

Jesus came to gather together those who had been dispersed (Mt 23:37) and lead them into the Kingdom of God (Lk 14:23; Mt 22:1-14). He proclaimed the New Covenant by His Word and His act of love at the Last Supper, but He was betrayed in His will to call people together: The assembly of the Twelve was dispersed (Mt 26:31; Mk 14:27). Yet He prayed for unity during His Passion (Jn 17:11-23) with loud cries and tears (Heb 5:7) and He was heard. In His Resurrection there was a "reconvocation" and it was now addressed to all human beings.

The Evangelists take great pains to show that the appearances of the Risen Lord are more than simple proofs of the Resurrection—they are indeed true and proper "assemblies." They always take place in the presence of the disciples gathered together (Lk 24:33; Jn 20:19; Ac 1:6; 2:1).

The one who calls the assemblies together is the Lord in person. "Behold, I am with you all days even to the end of the world" (Mt 28:20). Jesus also personally proclaims and interprets His Word (to the disciples at Emmaus—Lk 24:27; to the disciples in the Upper Room—Lk 24:44f). With this Word He enables the disciples to pass from unbelief to belief (Lk 24:25; Jn 20:24, 28f). Thus, the assembly of the Risen Christ is the place for an experience of faith in which human beings learn to go beyond sensible experience and encounter Christ the Lord.

The persons called together do not necessarily have faith. The Assembly can thereby become the place for the "reproach" that prompts conversion (Lk 24:25). The assembly is called to translate its faith in an act, proclaiming at the same time God's "wondrous deeds." For example, the disciples at Emmaus *recognized* Jesus in the breaking of the bread and they *recounted* the Good News of His Resurrection (Lk 25:30-35); Thomas *heeded* Christ's words to put his finger in his wounds and *publicly expressed* his faith: "My Lord and my God" (Jn 20:27f).

Such an act actuates the Covenant in the *today* (Lk 4:21) of the *assembly itself* (Jn 20:33; Ac 2:38; Mt 26:28; Jn 21:15-17). Salvation is now in action. Our Lord's farewell is no longer a leave-taking but a sending forth on mission to be "convokers" of the nations (Jn 20:21; Mk 16:15; Ac 1:8).

Then Pentecost (Ac 2) reproposes the assembly of the desert in a Christian key. God calls His Church from a condition of bondage ("fear of the Jews") and dispersion ("Parthians, Medes, and Elamites..."). The call is universal ("all the nations under heaven").

Those called are purified with wind and fire; the multitude is gathered together and listens to Peter's words which provide certain faith in Christ the Lord. The cultual action of the assembly is Baptism in the Name of Jesus Christ with the reception of the Spirit and the breaking of the Bread.

In the *today* of Pentecost are fulfilled God's promises "for you, for your children, and for those who are far off."

After Pentecost, the "model" of every Christian assembly will be the perseverance and assiduousness in the teaching of the Apostles, in common gatherings, in the Breaking of the Bread, and in prayer (Ac 2:42).

### The Liturgical Assembly Today

We are fortunate to be part of this assembly of the People of God today who can make the Eucharist the dialogue with God and our fellow Christians on this Sunday morning in this particular place. We must realize that the Eucharist is not something we "get something out of" but something we "bring something to"—our entire selves.

We are afflicted with a negative approach to the Eucharist and lament our boredom and aimlessness in it. Rather we should resolve to overcome such surface boredom by participating actively in what we are doing. We must strive to know what it is that we are doing, love what we know, and live what we love!

It does not matter whether we come from a homogeneous human community or whether we stem from diverse places, cultures, and ages; the people in our assembly do not constitute an amorphous crowd. We form an assembly, a people of God, gathered together in the name of the Father, the Son, and the Holy Spirit.

In the celebrant's greeting we discern the presence of the Risen Lord *among us*. We are purified by experiencing our "oneness" and we listen to the joyous announcement of the Word of salvation, which we acknowledge with faith. We become converted to God and to one another in the Prayer through the mediation of Christ and in the presentation of the gifts which symbolize our very selves.

These gifts are "taken" by the Father and "broken" and prepared during a solemn "thanksgiving" which recalls in particular the mystery of Christ's death and resurrection. They are offered to the Father and become the Body and Blood of Christ to be received in Communion by all. The Holy Spirit makes of the Church an Assembly-Body rendering continual thanksgiving to God.

The Eucharist gets its rhythm from our constant responses, especially the Amen, and makes us a multitude of "gatherers" in the life of each day, for the great Eucharistic assembly in heaven.

The assembly is a sacramental sign and functions as such a sign only when the members of the assembly actively carry out their respective roles. For the assembly is made up of priests as a result of Baptism and Holy Orders that the members have received.

Through Baptism all Christians are made priests capable of taking their rightful part in the Liturgy. They are deputed to make the liturgical action their own by internal and external participation—which must be active, full, and conscious. The same conclusion is also reached by considering the Liturgy's psychological efficacy on the individual participant. Without active participation, those who assist at the Liturgy do not receive the full psychological and moral effect of the Liturgy.

The Liturgy is an "epiphany" (a manifestation) of the Church. Therefore, it must possess a quality that is intrinsic to the nature of the Church. It must have a hierarchical structure. The Church is made up of members who differ in function and so is the liturgical assembly.

Today the Church has restored the active participation of the people (members of the assembly in the pews) which had been part of the early Liturgy but had fallen into disuse in the Middle Ages. Both St. Justin and St. Hippolytus (second century B.C.) wrote about the active participation of the people, their responses, and the clear distribution of roles in the Liturgy.

The faithful are to be present at the Eucharist and all liturgical rites with more than *devout attendance*. They are to be present with *active participation*.

> Mother Church earnestly desires that all the faithful should be led to that full, conscious, and active participation in liturgical celebrations which is demanded by the very nature of the Liturgy. Such participation by the Christian people as a "chosen race, a royal priesthood, a holy nation, a redeemed people" (1 P 2:9; cf. 2:4f), is their right and duty by reason of their Baptism.[6]

This participation must be both *internal and external*. The people must enlist not only minds and hearts in the service of God's worship but their bodies as well: tongues and lips, hands and feet, arms and legs, etc. For it is the whole person who is called upon to praise and glorify the Creator.

The surest way to achieve this active participation desired by the Church is to take one's rightful part in the celebration:

In the assembly which comes together to celebrate Mass, each person has the right and the duty to take an active part. However, the ways in which individuals do so vary according to the states and functions of each. All—whether clerics or lay people—should carry out their parts by doing all and only those parts which pertain to their office. In this way, the very organization of the celebration manifests the Church constituted in her various orders and ministries.[7]

### The People's Parts

The Church has done a masterful job in inserting meaningful and inspiring parts for the people all through the new rite of celebrating the Eucharist. Those who want to participate can do so to the fullest extent and become true co-celebrants with the priest simply by carrying out their parts.

The "new" Mass (like the "old") is composed of an *Ordinary* and a *Proper* (although the first is now called "Order"). The Ordinary can be thought of as the outline or framework of the structure of the Mass. It indicates what texts and ceremonies occur and the correct sequence which they should follow. It contains the texts that form part of almost every celebration.

The Proper contains the texts that vary according to the liturgical Seasons (Advent, Christmas, Lent and Easter, and Ordinary Time) or according to the particular feast (of a Saint who was a Martyr, or a Virgin, or a Doctor, etc.).

In both the Ordinary and the Proper there are texts and actions assigned to the different participants in the Eucharist, that is, to the celebrant, to the ministers, and to the people. This is the origin of the term *People's Parts*.

The Mass is divided into two logical components: the Liturgy of the Word of God and the Liturgy of the Eucharist. The word "Liturgy" is usually understood to mean "the work (role) of the People of God." In the Liturgy of the Word of God the people of God exercise their role by encountering Christ in the proclamation of the Word of God and by their preparation for, and response to that Word. In the Liturgy of the Eucharist the people exercise their role by actively participating in the renewal of the Sacrifice of

## The Role of the Liturgical Assembly

the Cross through their acclamations and responses as well as by their intimate union with the glorified Lord in Communion.

The Mass is further divided into five minor divisions—two in the Liturgy of the Word of God, and three in the Liturgy of the Eucharist. These are: (1) The Introductory Rites; (2) The Word of God; (3) The Preparation of the Gifts; (4) The Eucharistic Prayer; and (5) The Eucharistic Banquet. Each has its own specific function and particular message for the participants.

The Introductory Rites sets the tone for the entire celebration and is primarily a preparation for what follows. Its purpose is to create a unity of those who have come together in order to fashion a true Assembly made ready for meeting with Christ in the living proclamation of His Word and in the living Memorial of the Eucharistic Prayer, and for our intimate union with the Savior in the Eucharistic Banquet.

The Word of God brings Christ in our midst as our Teacher and Guide to the Father. It provides food for our mind as well by instilling in us the content of the Good News which our Lord came to proclaim to all human beings, and it calls for our positive response.

The Preparation of the Gifts serves as a kind of introduction to the Eucharistic part of the sacrifice. It enables us to make an offering of ourselves to the Father together with the gift of His Son (symbolized by the bread and wine which will soon be consecrated).

The Eucharistic Prayer is the great consecratory prayer of praise and thanksgiving to the Father in living Memorial of Christ's Death, Resurrection and Ascension, and specifically of His actions of the Last Supper. We encounter Christ; and through, with, and in Him Who becomes present among us in a real and wonderful way we render to the Father all honor and glory.

The Eucharistic Banquet represents the completion of the sacrifice and the highlight of our participation. We are joined in intimate *union* with our Savior by the reception of Communion, the Food our Father gives us to nourish us on our way to Him. This is the sacred banquet of God's children, in which the Memorial of Christ is renewed, our souls are filled with grace, and a pledge of future glory in heaven is given.

The Ordinary People's Parts occur throughout every division of the Mass, and the Proper People's Parts occur in all except the Eucharistic Prayer, which is the priestly prayer par excellence. Furthermore, these parts are so structured as to elicit definite sentiments from the people and insure the full participation on the part of the assembly.

## The Introductory Rites—Keynote

The Entrance hymn (and Entrance antiphon which is substituted when there is no singing) is usually regarded as setting the tone for the particular celebration of the day. We acclaim Jesus (in the person of the priest) who comes to reenact and re-present His saving Sacrifice for us and to invite us to partake of His sacrificial Meal—to become one in Him.

In the Ordinary parts that follow, we exchange greetings with the priest, and ask God to purify us before we hear His Word and celebrate His Eucharist. At the same time, through this Penitential rite we ask forgiveness of one another so that we will offer this Eucharist with complete solidarity.

Now we turn our attention to *praise* and *thanksgiving* in beautiful and ancient Ordinary texts in praise of Christ: the Kyrie, a litany-like plea to Christ (which because of its structure can also be used in the Penitential rite) and the Gloria, which is addressed to the Father and concludes with praise to the Trinity, but its corpus is a lyrical praise of the Incarnate Son, our Redeemer and our Intercessor with the Father.

The Introductory Rites comes to a close with the celebrant reciting a Prayer in the name of the people, who by their response—*"Amen"*—assent to all that has gone before. This prayer gathers together the sentiments expressed in the Entrance Antiphon (and hymn) and recasts them into a formal petition to the Father in the name of the People of God relying on the merits of Christ His Son.

## The Word of God—Response

Christ now comes in our midst in the proclamation of the Word of God. The people have an Ordinary response after each of the three readings and two proper chants that used to be called intervenient and are now known as the Responsorial Psalm and the Alleluia or Gospel Acclamation.

The Responsorial Psalm is a response to the First Reading (usually taken from the Prophets of the Old Testament or the Letters of the Apostles of the New Testament). It constitutes a sure way of making a positive response to the Word we have just heard.

The Alleluia looks forward to the Gospel message. It is an acclamation for the Christ Who comes among us during the proclamation of God's Word. It forms the people's culmination of the Liturgy of the Word of God—short, yet packed with meaning.

Liturgists traditionally regarded these "intervenient chants" as the most important Proper Parts of the People, since they are directly responsive and introductory to God's Word which is the highlight of the first major division of Mass.

The Assembly now goes to meet Christ as He becomes present once again in the proclamation of His Gospel. The second dialogue-response of the people at this point bears this out: "Glory to You, Lord."

After listening reverently to God's Word, the people listen to the updating of that Word (to the here and now) by the Homily that is preached. They then voice their acceptance of this Word in the Nicene Creed—a long and beautiful profession of faith that is one of the People's Parts of the Ordinary, and dates back to the 11th century.

Here too prayers are interspersed relating this part of the Mass to actual circumstances; these are the so-called Prayer of the Faithful. Ideally, the list of petitions should take its starting point from the Scripture texts just proclaimed and the response just recited. The people can then readily give their assent to these sentiments by the *Amen* at the end of the concluding prayer said by the celebrant.

### The Preparation of the Gifts—Offering

The second major division of Mass also begins with a processional chant which introduces the Preparation of the Gifts. Originally, the text was made up of an antiphon and psalm like the *Entrance Antiphon*. While the gifts of bread and wine (and other goods) were received by the celebrant, the people used to sing the antiphon and as many verses of the psalm as were needed to fill up the time required.

However, as the procession fell into disuse when gifts were no longer provided by the people, the psalm lost its reason for being and itself disappeared into history. What remained was merely a truncated form of the antiphon. In the new rite even the antiphon has been put to rest and replaced by an Offertory hymn.

This hymn sets the tone for the Preparation of the Gifts. It is sung while a few members of the assembly are bringing the gifts to the altar from which the Sacrifice of the Mass will be effected—the bread and wine as well as the sacred vessels. They are our gifts to God which will be turned into His Gift (Jesus) to us.

These gifts encompass not only the sacred vessels and utensils that are brought up; they also embody all the monetary gifts that we offer for the good of the community (for Liturgy, counseling, education, etc.). Perhaps most important of all, they also embrace all the joys and sorrows that the present day or present week will bring for us and the community as a whole.

We symbolically place them in the hands of those in the Offertory Procession to bring them to the altar, to be offered in our name in this Holy Sacrifice. In this way, we will be able to go on in our pilgrim journey fortified by the graces Jesus has gained for us.

Just before the end of this part, the celebrant exhorts the people to join wholeheartedly in his sacrifice and theirs. They immediately give their affirmative response—vocalizing what they have already symbolized in the Offertory Procession.

Finally, the celebrant adds the "summing up" Prayer over the Gifts in the name of the whole Assembly. It is usually related to the Offertory Hymn, and the people give their firm approval to all that has gone before with their Amen.

## The Eucharistic Prayer—Encounter

Although the whole Mass is a remembrance, a commemoration, a memorial, a re-presentation of the Passion, Death, Resurrection, and Ascension of Jesus, it is in the Eucharistic Prayer that this Paschal Mystery is *fully* recalled and re-presented. By participating actively in this Prayer, we really relive the whole of Sacred History; our faith is restored and we receive an incomparable degree of strength and comfort.

At first glance it looks as if the people have little to do at this crucial part of the Mass. For the Eucharistic Prayer is uniquely the prayer of the president of the assembly, who voices the thanksgiving in the name of the people.

A closer look dispels this impression, and shows the beautiful dialogue that runs throughout the prayer, enabling the people to take a fully active part in it. Ultimately, this dialogue leads the people to encounter the Lord in His saving deeds through this redemptive sacrifice. At this time, there are Ordinary parts for the people.

The Eucharistic Prayer opens with an Introductory Dialogue that helps the assembly get into the spirit of the Canon. We are invited to praise and thank God; we give our prompt response that it is not only good, but right to do so.

The Preface follows, with the celebrant delineating the particular reason for praising God on the day in question—in addition to the overriding reasons found in Salvation History. At the end we join our sentiments to those found in the Preface by voicing another praise of God with the magnificent Holy, Holy, Holy. We stress that the earth as well as heaven is filled with the glory of God and it will be more filled with glory as we continue our Eucharist.

We go on to join the celebrant silently as he calls upon the Holy Spirit to make holy our Sacrifice, and we enter the narrative of the Last Supper. By it we, so to speak, are given a front seat at the Last Supper. The celebrant in Christ's person repeats the words and actions of Christ, allowing us to encounter Jesus at the high point of His sacrificial giving on earth.

Christ becomes present in a new and wonderful way, and we address Him in the beautiful words of the Memorial Acclamation. We should strive to pronounce them with outward reverence and inner conviction. They constitute what the Mass is all about. Christ has redeemed us *in history*, is with us now in *mystery* and will come to us in *glory*. It is our little Easter.

The Eucharistic Prayer recalls the saving events of Christ and then stipulates the "us" for whom the Sacrifice is being offered: the servants of God, our relatives, friends, and benefactors who are Christians as well as all people, living and dead.

Then the Solemn Conclusion gives glory to the Father, through the Son, in the Holy Spirit. We rise and utter our wholehearted endorsement of this sentiment through our Great Amen. It gives our reaction to the offering that has been made. We want to offer ourselves with, through, and in Christ and we eagerly look forward to our union with Him in Communion.

**The Eucharistic Banquet—Union**

This final major division of Mass is again governed by the people's processional chant which this time does not introduce it. The people prepare for Communion by reciting their Ordinary Parts: the Lord's Prayer, the responses to the Prayer for Peace, the Sign of Peace, and the Lamb of God (a prayer for pardon and peace), while the celebrant makes a quiet preparation for Communion. Then both celebrant and people acknowledge their unworthiness to receive such a Visitor in the words of the Centurion of the Gospel: "Lord, I am not worthy. . . ."

At this point the third Processional Chant is recited by the people. Once

Chapter 3

# BIBLE AND LITURGY: CHRIST'S PRESENCE IN THE WORD

We are living today in the greatest "communication explosion" the world has ever known. All sorts of technical gadgets are at our fingertips for instant communication and information-gathering. Our world has truly become a global village. It has, so to speak, shrunk so that we can be present to all other people and communicate with them.

Communication requires some kind of personal presence. We communicate through words and signs. Human beings are characterized by their ability to create symbols and to think in terms of them. The very languages by which we communicate are symbolic—"symbolic codes," in the words of Bernard Lee.[8]

Even as the adherents of logical positivism, logical empiricism, and linguistic analysis[9] have been steadily constricting human efforts to communicate through spoken language by impugning its universal sign-value, a new group of scholars has been uncovering the value of body language. Researchers at the University of California at Santa Cruz have shown that nonverbal communication is a much more reliable instrument than verbal communication. And this nonverbal communication is based on universally accepted body signs and gestures—body language.[10]

We are able to read and perform many nonverbal scripts, although we would be hard pressed to explain how we know their meaning. Without our fluency in nonverbal communication the simplest everyday interaction—knowing when to speak in conversation—would be awkward or even impossible. Human beings are social animals who must communicate with one another in order to survive. Communication of any reality is based on signs (bodily or otherwise) or symbols (verbal or otherwise). We communicate not only with words but with our entire body as well. Our body "is the first word that every man pronounces; it belongs in fact to the 'order of language.' "[11] Ultimately, it is the human person who communicates, the whole person with all its qualities and experiences. No one communicates in a vacuum. All of us communicate with our mind, body, and emotions.

We use signs and symbols (in the broadest sense of those terms) to communicate with others. The necessity of signs and symbols is axiomatic. Ian Ramsey has shown that even in science the language utilized never achieves complete identity—there is always something deeper that is not communicated by the simple recital of facts but goes beyond them. There is a kind of mystery.[12]

In making a hypothesis or a law, the scientist goes beyond the facts; he makes use of disclosures that are based on the facts but surpass them. He is thus using imagistic or symbolic language. This is undoubtedly the reason why the use of models or images has become so prevalent in our day in the natural sciences, social sciences, and systems analysis.

Religious thought, on the contrary, deals by nature with mysteries that are even more inaccessible to human understanding than are the mysteries of the physical universe. God, soul, grace, and Church are among topics that human beings cannot immediately apprehend or imagine. Hence, they must be described in terms of signs, symbols, or myths—that is, by images that can approximate the reality to be transmitted and at the same time leave room for the mystery.

Traditionally, there have been three sources for sacred signs: creation (the so-called vestiges of God), historical and supernatural revelation (culminated by Jesus Christ), and the period of the Church (Saints, Liturgy, events of daily life). Thus, almost anything can be used to communicate religious truths:

> Images . . . speak to man existentially and find an echo in the inarticulate depths of his psyche. Such images communicate through their evocative power. They convey a latent meaning that is apprehended in a nonconceptual, even a subliminal, way. Symbols transform the horizons of man's life, integrate his perception of reality, alter his scale of values, reorient his loyalties, attachments, and aspirations in a manner far exceeding the powers of abstract conceptual thought.[13]

### God's Word in Human Beings

Left to themselves, human beings cannot discover all the mysteries of God or His creatures. In His goodness, God has revealed to us many things about Himself and the world. This revelation has taken place in time. God intervened in human history and communicated His merciful plans to human beings.

The record of this self-communication of God is contained in the Bible (the Word of God). It is a record of a message and events. God spoke and acted in this communication—word and event went together. He also inspired the sacred authors of the books of the Bible to the extent that He is the principal author.

This does not mean, that the sacred authors were merely secretaries to whom God dictated. Neither does it mean that the human authors had no say in the contents and distinctive style of the books. In reality, they are true authors, utilizing all their faculties—intellect, imagination, and will—to communicate a revelation of God.

The revelation of God in the Bible comes to us in a manner that is in common use among human beings. Just as the Word of God became Man in all things except sin (Heb 4:15), so God's words, spoken by human tongues, have taken on all the qualities of human language except error.

The entire Bible is absolutely true—but it is true in the sense in which each kind of literary form bears witness to it. "Truth is proposed and expressed in a variety of ways, depending on whether a text is history of one kind or another or whether its form is that of prophecy, poetry or another type of speech."[14]

Distinctions of form and structure appear in all human communication. We have prose and poetry. We also have more specific forms, such as epic, lyric, and dramatic poetry and narrative, rhetorical, and expository prose. In each of these the "truth" of an event or subject is presented in a different fashion—one that is in keeping with its purpose and method—but it is still the truth.

In order to understand the Bible correctly, we must do what we do in ordinary life. We must know the specific literary form of each book and narrative and extract the particular type of truth such a form is intended to impart. We must interpret correctly the particular type of communication it is giving us—as we do with all other human communications.[15]

## God's Word in the Church

In our world there is a preponderance of words. A sea of words flows daily and threatens to inundate and deafen us—words that are written, spoken, and even shouted. Yet there is really only one decisive Word, the Word that God addresses to human beings to initiate a dialogue with them, to establish a community of life. This is the only word that is capable of imparting light and life.

This Word comes to us in the Bible which has been preserved for us by the Church. But this Word is not something dead—it is a living reality. Truth entails a past, a present, and a future.

The Church owes her very existence to this Word. She is a people brought together in the unity of the Father, the Son, and the Holy Spirit by the proclamation of the Word through the Apostles in the past.

This convocation made by God in Christ is a mystery that continues in the present time. The History of Salvation is now to construct progressively the Kingdom of God and widen its dimensions to the ends of the world.

The means for this is always the proclamation of the Good News. It is this which makes the Church. In her adherence to the Word of God the Church attains a unity of faith regardless of all barriers of nations, races, and civilizations, and becomes an apostolic Church.

This Word of God lives and grows in the Church. It is a mystery of revelation, something that surpasses us on every side and that our human mind is incapable of embracing in all its meaning. The Mystery of the Word is in some sense inexhaustible.

The Church transmits a Word that is no static word but a Word that grows and is stretched to a fulfillment. It is a living Word that creates a community and makes it the carrier of the salvific proclamation. The creative Word of God uttered at the beginning of time and bringing forth the entire universe has become the re-creating and regenerating Word of God in the process of salvation.

In the Old Testament it was the Word of Creation and the Word of the Covenant that established the universe, called the human race into existence, and held the people of Israel together.

The history of the Israelites in Egypt, the self-revelation of God to Moses in the burning bush (Ex 3), and the Covenant in the desert (Ex 16-31) are classical examples of the mysterious power of God's Word.

To hear that Word, Israel had to be called together (Dt 31:10-12; 2 K 23; Ne 8:9). Listening to the Word led naturally to an explanation of the Word (1 K 8:23; 2 K 8:9f), and then to a profession of faith (Dt 27:14-26).

In the New Testament, the tone is set by Jesus' mission itself: "Let us go elsewhere to the neighboring country towns, so that I can preach there too because that is why I have come" (Mk 1:38).

Jesus also said: "I tell you most solemnly, whoever listens to My words, and believes in the One Who sent Me . . ." (Jn 5:24). He thus made the Word a medium of God's communication to human beings and of their ascent to God (Jn 6:45).

He told the Apostles to preach the Word to the whole world (Mt 28:18) and the Acts of the Apostles is eloquent testimony to the wondrous working of the Word of God through the preaching of the Apostles.

The Word of God is still present today in the world and acts in the Church in many ways. The living Church is thus the sole interpreter of the Bible, for it is the Church who through her faith knows what the Bible intends to say at its deepest level—beyond the letter and its purely historical meaning.

This does not mean that the Church controls the Bible and can manipulate it at will. On the contrary, the life of the Church has its foundation in the witness that the Church born of the Christian event gives in the Bible. This witness continually confronts, challenges, and moves her to renewal and conversion.

The Christian Bible is founded on the Church and the Church is founded on the Bible. Both are ultimately founded on Jesus Christ and on the Father Who raised Him from the dead. The Bible is the foundational and normative witness; the Church is the continuing life of this witness.

### God's Word in the Liturgy

The Word of God acts in the Church in many ways—through private Bible reading, for example, and even through other people. However, it is especially in the Liturgy that the Word is present and active. It is here that the Church realizes herself, becomes most completely what she is.

The privileged place for proclaiming the Bible is the confessing and celebrating community of the Mystery of Salvation. For it was in the confessing and celebrating community that the Bible had its origin and took its most profound life. First it was through the Old Testament, in the liturgy, in the synagogal reading, study, and prayer; then through the words of the New Testament, in the proclamations and the Liturgy of the Church.

Through the exegesis of the Liturgy, the Bible rediscovers its vitality and actuality. It ceases to be a simple story of the past and becomes *my story*. The promises of God made to His people are promises made also *to me*; the prayer of the people of God becomes *my prayer*; the wondrous works of God in favor of His people are renewed *on my behalf*.

The Liturgy may be viewed as a dialogue, an exchange of words between God and His people. But it is even more—it is an action in which God acts and the people become involved. In this communication, the Liturgy makes use of signs as well as words. It requires bodily attitudes, comprises gestures and actions, makes use of things, is carried out in places, confects objects and consecrates them.

Some of these signs are natural, reproducing the language that God has, as it were, inserted in creation and the human heart. But most are Biblical signs: those that Jesus Himself used for the Mass and the Sacraments as well as those that the rest of the Scriptures show us being used by our predecessors in the Faith.

The Liturgy has been called the *Bible in action* for the Bible permeates every part of the Church's liturgical rites. The Liturgy is made up of Biblical passages (readings), Biblical chants (antiphons), Biblical formulas (greetings, acclamations, and institution narrative), Biblical allusions (prayers), and Biblical instruction (homily).

Liturgy represents the perfect forum for God's Word to be proclaimed, understood, and loved. It presents the true background for the interpretation and appreciation of God's Word. That is why in the new Liturgy of the Mass the Church has brought the Liturgy of the Word into closer relationship with the Liturgy of the Eucharist and has increased the number of Scripture readings.

### Christ's Presence in the Word

The Liturgy makes Christ present to us. This is not a *local* presence, a simple accident of space that involves no interrelation with us. It is a substantial presence of heart, mind and will. It enables us to be united with Christ *personally*.

Thus we are empowered to enter into the event of Jesus' sacrificial Death and Glorification which breaks the bonds of time and is accessible to people of every era. By participating actively, consciously, and fully in the liturgical celebrations of the Church, we attain the salvation wrought by God in Christ.

The Second Vatican Council spelled out four types of presence of Christ in the Liturgy. Each takes place for a specific reason and in a different way.[16]

(1) *Christ's Presence in His Ministers at Mass or in the Sacraments.* This presence links us with the fruits of our Lord's salvation. It constitutes

our encounter of Christ today in order to realize His saving effect in our lives. We are inserted into the Paschal Mystery of Jesus that took place once and for all some 2,000 years ago in His Passion, Death, and Resurrection.

(2) *Christ's Presence in the Assembly.* In accord with Christ's promise, wherever two or three of His followers are gathered in His Name, He is there with them—as their Friend and Intercessor with the Father. When we gather to accomplish the Eucharistic Sacrifice or the Sacraments—which are the Greatest Prayer and its offshoots respectively—Jesus prays with us: "He prays for us and prays in us; He prays for us as our Priest and He prays in us as our Friend" (St. Augustine).

(3) *Christ's Presence under the Eucharistic Signs of Bread and Wine.* This is known as the presence of Christ par excellence, His Real Presence. One of the reasons for this is that it is the only one that remains. The Bread and Wine remain the Body and Blood, Soul and divinity of Christ as long as they last after they are consecrated.

This presence is intended to be the means for our close union with Jesus in His sacrifice and also our union with our brothers and sisters who share that presence with us. It provides our entrance into the Sacred Banquet in which the living Memory of Christ's Passion is recalled, our souls are filled with grace, and we receive a pledge of future glory.

(4) *Christ's Presence in the Proclamation of the Word of God.* Jesus is the Word of God Himself and the Author of all Revelation. Hence, it is actually He Himself Who speaks to us when the Sacred Scriptures are liturgically proclaimed. He becomes present among us when the Old and the New Testament are read.

However, Jesus is most present when the Gospel is proclaimed. He is as present to us as He was to the people who gathered to hear Him along the roads of Palestine. He comes to us as our Teacher Who leads us to Him Who is all Truth.

### The Reading as Salvific Event

Admittedly, few Catholics have had enough liturgical catechesis to be able to say that they co-celebrate the Eucharist with the celebrant—and this is an important lack. However, even fewer would think of Christ's presence in His Word as counterbalancing Christ's presence in His Sacrament,[17]—and this is just as important a lack. As the Church has indicated, the Liturgy of the Word and the Liturgy of the Eucharist go together, and the same is true of Christ's presence in each.

Yet the average Catholic knows little of this, indeed, the very appearance of the Liturgy of the Word in most celebrations expresses the idea that it is not very important. The readings or proclamations all too often seem to be an exercise in futility: the readers are frequently mediocre, the acoustics are poor, and the texts themselves are akin to a reading lesson. In no way do they resemble a proclamation making Christ present personally to the Assembly at worship.

Catholics have never been schooled in this type of Liturgy. We have no tradition (at least in the twentieth century Western Church) of viewing public proclamation of Scripture in this way. We have to work at it.

Another negating factor is televison. We are accustomed to having highly trained announcers and news people come into our living rooms, as well as gifted actors and actresses, communicating with us in a professional manner. Their diction, comportment, and interpretation of written texts are superb.

In the light of such "natural" performances, the rendition of the readers at Mass is easily outclassed. There are exceptions of course. It is a delight to hear an intelligent and convincing proclamation of the Good News, but many lectors seem amateurish. It is natural, then, to give short shrift to their performance and be little concerned with the enormous pageantry of the event that is taking place in our presence.

The liturgical reading is an event, a happening—even more, it is a *salvific event*. No matter how amateurish it may be, no matter how distracting, no matter how disappointing, it nonetheless brings before us the Word God wants to *speak to us today*. It enables us to encounter God today!

> The multiform riches contained in the one Word of God are wondrously brought out in the different types of liturgical celebrations and liturgical assemblies. This occurs when the unfolding Mystery of Christ is recalled during the course of the Liturgical Year, when the Sacraments and Sacramentals of the Church are celebrated, or when the faithful each respond to the inner workings of the Holy Spirit within them. For then the liturgical celebration, which is based primarily on the Word of God and sustained by it, becomes a new event and enriches that Word with new meaning and power. Thus in the Liturgy the Church faithfully follows the way of reading and interpreting the Holy Scriptures which Christ Himself—beginning

with the "today" of His coming forward [in the synagogue at Capernaum]—urged all to use in searching the Scriptures.[18]

Non-Catholic Christians have a tradition of seeing Christ in His Word. They are accustomed to viewing Scripture as God's Word to us today. Catholics have lost that tradition in recent centuries and are just recapturing it now.[19] But it will take a long time for such an attitude to become second nature to us.

Until it does become embedded in our religious consciousness, the only way we can appreciate the Liturgy of the Word is by making a dedicated effort to view it with *faith*. It is faith that tells us that God speaks to us today through His Prophets and Apostles whose words are proclaimed at Mass and through His Son whose deeds and words are set forth in the Gospel proclamation.

It is faith that shows us Christ's presence among us through the power of His words and deeds. He is as present to us as He was to His Apostles and disciples on earth.

It is faith that emphasizes the saving event of Christ's presence among us and God's intervention in our lives. The person of faith discerns the realities in the proclamation of the Word and is enabled to live God's salvific events to the full.

To the person bereft of this discerning faith, the Liturgy of the Word is merely an exercise in reading—and a rather poor one at that! The same effect could be obtained by a private reading of the Scriptures proclaimed!

### God's Word Must Be Made Intelligible

Most of us have probably had the thought: "If only I had been able to meet Christ on earth and listen to His words . . . what great faith I would have!"

There is a good deal of truth to such a thought, but there is also another side to it. In order to be reached by Christ's words, we would have needed to be prepared. We would have needed to obey the "rules" for humanly understanding Christ at that time.

For example, it would have been of little value for us to hear Jesus if we did not *know* Aramaic, the language He spoke; or if we did not *listen* to His words; or if we could not *physically* hear Him. In other words, in order to really dialogue with someone we need to obey the laws of communication.

Thus, in order for us to encounter Christ in the Word today, we need to make that word intelligible to us. We need to become familiar with its language *beforehand*. The more we read over the Readings before Mass, the more understandable they will be to us at the Liturgy of the Word and the greater appreciation we will have of Christ's presence in each particular Word.

A genuine familiarity with the Word of God will enable us to take better advantage of one of the outstanding qualities of that Word—its endless meanings. No matter how often we hear it, we always come to it anew. We can never exhaust what God is telling us in it.

For example, the Gospel for the Twenty-Ninth Sunday in Ordinary Time for Year A is Mt 22:15-21, which speaks of giving to Caesar what is Caesar's and to God what is God's.

We are well aware that our circumstances are no longer what they were for the people of God in Jesus' day. Christ is telling us to give to government what is legitimately government's—and that can only be decided ultimately by the people in our system of government, which is one *of* the people, *by* the people, and *for* the people.

Note the difference in nuance in the teaching. In Jesus' day government ruled and the people had to give government what it ruled. In our situation, it is the people themselves who rule, so to speak, and we are called to give what we the people decide through those who represent us. The underlying idea is that we need law to live in society. This remains for all ages.

Thus, Jesus' Word is adaptable to all peoples and all societies. It is living and more effective than a two-edged sword. For it preaches the truth that makes us free.

The Word of God unceasingly calls to mind and extends the plan of salvation, which achieves its fullest expression in the Liturgy. Accordingly, the liturgical celebration becomes the continuing, complete, and effective presentation of God's Word.

That Word continually proclaimed in the Liturgy is thus always a living, active Word through the power of the Holy Spirit. It expresses the Father's love that never fails to have its effect on us.[20]

**God's Word Calls for a Positive Response**

We are not speaking here of purely individualistic encounters. We do not receive a message that is solely our own. We encounter God and Christ *in the Church*. We receive a message that is for us within the context of the

Christian community which is the Church. We are enabled to perceive God's presence, and to understand His message to us today, *only through the medium of the Church.*

Anyone who wants to understand the event and the message must do so in union with the Church. We must listen with the Church if we would hear God's true Word. Most important, from a subjective point of view, God's Word calls for a response on our part. Without a response it would be meaningless for us to listen to that Word. The sole reason that it is pronounced is to elicit a response.

We are called to *respond positively* to that Word. We must embrace it with an open mind and heart. It may call us to make sacrifices that we do not enjoy. Yet we must follow through and respond in conscience to it.

This is part of the implicit commitment we make when we assent to become a member of the Assembly that comes to celebrate the Eucharist—to celebrate this Word and this Sacrament. This is what Father Gerard Sloyan is referring to when he stresses in a popular book on Liturgy that the Eucharist must change us.

Whether we like it or not, this is the end result of every Eucharist. Those who celebrate it with full, active, and conscious participation are changed in some way. They are renewed, taken out of some aspect of themselves and made better.

If we give the Liturgy a chance, this will happen to us too. Of course, it will not happen completely all at once. It will happen imperceptibly over a period of time. With each Eucharist we celebrate with the proper sentiments, we will come closer to the person that God wants us to be. We will be putting on Christ—taking on in our own inimitable way His attitude, His eyes, His ears.

We will then begin to see our lives in the light of God's eternal plan. We will begin to do the task that He has set out for us, a task that is ours alone and no one else's.

> When God shares his Word with us, He awaits our response, that is, our listening and our worship "in Spirit and in truth" (Jn 4:23). The Holy Spirit makes our response effective, so that we carry out in our lives what we hear in the celebration of the Liturgy: "Be doers of the Word and not hearers only" (Jm 1:22).
>
> The liturgical celebration and the faithful's participation receive outward expression in actions, gestures, and words. These derive their full meaning not merely from their origin in human experience but from their point of reference: the Word of God and the economy

of salvation. Hence, the participation of the faithful in the Liturgy increases to the extent that while listening to the Word of God spoken in the Liturgy they strive more diligently to commit themselves to the Word of God made flesh in Christ. They endeavor to conform their lives to what they celebrate in the Liturgy, and then in turn to incorporate in the celebration of the Liturgy everything that they do in their lives.[21]

Chapter 4
# THE EUCHARIST:
# SACRIFICE, MEMORIAL, AND PRESENCE

Today it is not very fashionable to ask: "What is the Mass essentially?" Presumably everyone knows what it is. After all, everything is now in English. How could anyone fail to know what the Mass is? Unfortunately, the opposite is the case in most instances—how can people know what the Mass is when they are no longer taught its essence in a detailed way?

What did Jesus want to be done when He said: "Do this in memory of Me"? Only when we know the answer to this can we hope to know the proper fundamental attitude that should be ours at Mass—whether it be that of the officiating ordained priest or that of the co-celebrating faithful who are asked to participate in the service.

No single word fully indicates what the Mass is and what riches it contains. Our term "Mass" in itself is inadequate, for it originally meant the dismissal of some or all participants in a religious sense. That is why today it is called a Meal, a Celebration, the Liturgy, the Eucharist (which means thanksgiving), and the Holy Sacrifice. It is a Memorial—in the sense of a re-presentation of the Sacrifice of Calvary.

The Mass is a meeting of the Divine and the human, of eternity and time, of the past and the present. Heaven and earth come together in this celebration and the principal actors are unseen: the unique High Priest and Victim Jesus Christ, the Holy Spirit, and the Heavenly Father.

The Mass is the action of the Head of the Mystical Body but also of His members. It is a cooperation of the visible ordained priest and the Christians who in virtue of their Baptism share the "general" or "common" priesthood of the people of God.

Thus, the Mass is a Re-presentation, a true Sacrifice, a Meal, of the Passion, Death and Resurrection of Christ. Through the hands of the priest

Christ renews the offering He made when He accomplished once and for all the bloody Sacrifice on Calvary.

The Mass is the Memorial of the Lord in the Biblical sense of that term—recalling the past in such a way as to make it present for us. At Mass, our Redemption is constantly worked out, for the Christ Who is made present distributes and applies to His Church the treasures of Redemption.

The Second Vatican Council says: "Our Savior at the Last Supper, the night He was betrayed, instituted the Eucharistic Sacrifice of His Body and His Blood, in order to perpetuate the Sacrifice of the Cross through the centuries, until He comes, and by this to give to the Church, His well-beloved spouse, the memorial of His death and His resurrection."[22]

The Memorial of the Passion makes us participate in the very fruits of the Passion. It is not enough to say that the Mass is a Sacrifice of Praise and Thanksgiving (see Rm 12). The Mass is certainly that—but it is also infinitely more.

The Mass is more than a simple commemoration, a simple recalling of the Sacrifice that was accomplished on the Cross. It is a propitiatory Sacrifice, for the work of our salvation is really exercised and accomplished in it.

Vatican II has made very clear that there are two forms of priesthood in the Church to carry out the Sacrifice left us by Jesus—the ministerial priesthood and the common priesthood or priesthood of the faithful. This has always been a teaching of the Church but it had become obscured in recent times. It stems from the celebrated Scripture passage from the First Epistle of Peter (2:9):

"You . . . are a chosen race, *a royal priesthood*, a holy nation, a people He claims for His own to proclaim the glorious works of the One Who called you from darkness into His marvelous light."

These two types of priesthood differ from one another in essence as well as in degree but they are also interrelated. Each of them in its own way is a participation in the *One* Priesthood of Christ. Each of them has its own role to play in accomplishing the Sacrifice of Christ.

The ministerial priest, by the sacred power he enjoys, molds and rules the priestly people. He confects the Eucharistic Sacrifice in the Person of Christ and offers it to God in the name of the whole people. They join the offering of the faithful to the Sacrifice of the Head.

Until the Second Coming of our Lord, ministerial priests re-present and apply in the Sacrifice of the Mass the One Sacrifice of the New Covenant.

## The Eucharist: Sacrifice, Memorial, and Presence

This is the Sacrifice of Christ offering Himself once and for all to the Father as the spotless Victim.

The Eucharistic Prayer, which is the heart of the Eucharistic Celebration, belongs solely to the ordained priest. The people unite with him silently and show their assent by the three Acclamations (see below).

The priesthood of the faithful enables them to unite themselves, with the whole Church, to the offering which the Lord makes of Himself to His Father, to make it their own, and to integrate their own offering in it: "Taking part in the Eucharistic Sacrifice, which is the fount and apex of the whole Christian life, they offer the Divine Victim to God, and offer themselves along with it."[23]

"The Church, earnestly desires that Christ's faithful when present at this Mystery of Faith, should be there not as strangers or silent spectators. On the contrary, through a proper appreciation of the rites and prayers they should participate knowingly, devoutly, and actively.

"They should . . . be refreshed at the Table of the Lord's Body; they should give thanks to God; by offering the Immaculate Victim, not only through the hands of the priest, but also with him, they should learn to offer themselves too. Through Christ the Mediator, they should be drawn day by day into ever closer union with God and with each other, so that finally God may be all in all."[24]

Everything in the lives of the faithful—activities, prayers, apostolic undertakings, daily labors, trials—become spiritual offerings, pleasing to God through Jesus Christ. During the Celebration of the Eucharist, these sacrifices are most lovingly offered to the Father along with the Lord's Body.

### The People's Acclamations

A most important vehicle for the carrying out of the people's common priesthood in the Mass is the implementation of their acclamations during the Eucharistic Prayer. These enable the people to take full part in the Eucharistic and Sacrificial Prayer of the priest. They are of the utmost importance in helping them unite with the Offering of Jesus made by the priest in their name and the name of the whole Church.

*The Holy, Holy, Holy (or "Sanctus").* After giving their assent to praise God by the Introductory Dialogue to the Eucharistic Prayer, the people come in again after the Preface has succinctly outlined the reasons for this praise *today*. They thus praise God for the particular Mystery of the History of Salvation that is being celebrated on a given day or Season.

The principal way they do this is by the Acclamation: *Holy, Holy, Holy*. It comes from Isaiah 6:3 (with an allusion to Dn 7:10) and is our way of showing the unity of our Sacrifice of Praise with that of the Angels and Saints in heaven.

A second part follows, which begins and ends with the words "Hosanna in the highest" and "Blessed is He Who comes in the Name of the Lord." This shows that our Sacrifice is above all a Sacrifice of praise. We lose ourselves in the Divine Majesty and at the same time offer ourselves and every aspect of our lives to God.

*The Memorial Acclamation*. The whole Mass is an *anamnesis*, a memorial and re-presentation of the passion and death, resurrection and ascension of Jesus. This is the Paschal Mystery, and it is especially recalled in a unique and living way by the Eucharistic Prayer.

As we listen to the priest proclaim this Prayer, we must make it our own as well. Then we will really re-live the whole of Sacred History. Our faith will be restored and we will receive an incomparable degree of strength and comfort.

To aid us in acquiring these sentiments the Church has given us an integral part at the very high point of the Eucharistic Prayer. After the Consecration, we are called to unite ourselves to the whole economy of salvation, the entire plan of God's love, for the world: "Let us recall the Mystery of Salvation." We can do so by pronouncing—both outwardly and inwardly—one of the four formulas of the Memorial Acclamation:

(1) Christ has died,/Christ is risen,/Christ will come again. (2) Dying you destroyed our death,/rising you restored our life./Lord Jesus, come in glory. (3) When we eat this Bread and drink this Cup,/we proclaim your death, Lord Jesus,/until you come in glory. (4) Lord, by your cross and resurrection/you have set us free./ You are the Savior of the world.

By this Memorial Acclamation, we celebrate the wondrous reality that Christ has redeemed us, is with us now to apply that Redemption to each of us, and will return in glory to bring that Redemption to perfection for all.

*The Great Amen*. At the conclusion of the Eucharistic Prayer the Church again makes the people intervene with external demonstration of their internal union with the Memorial that has taken place. She gives us the Great Amen to say or sing.

The conclusion of the Eucharistic Prayer is a solemn proclamation of glory to the Father, through the Son, in the Holy Spirit—which is known as a Doxology. It proclaims that glory in virtue of the whole plan of salvation that has been recalled and made present for us in our Eucharist, and applied to this assembly here and now.

What is more natural than the fact that we should give a ringing affirmation of this praise of God for His goodness and wondrous deeds! We say—through our Amen—that we heartily approve what has been done in this Eucharistic Action in our name. We also show concretely that we have been part of the Thanksgiving and the Offering of Christ that have taken place.

St. Augustine tells us that saying *Amen* is like putting our signature to the Eucharistic Prayer. We should, therefore, express it with understanding, sincerity, and devotion. It is our way of making every Eucharist our own by placing our stamp of approval on it.

### The Lord's Presence

The Eucharist is also a Presence—the Presence of the Risen Jesus to His Church. This Presence is effected in both parts of the Liturgical Celebration: the Liturgy of the Word and the Liturgy of the Eucharist. In both of these Christ is present under symbols.

There are two tables of the Lord—the table of the Word and the table of the Eucharist. At the first, Jesus is present under the Veil of the words that impart the Word of God and at the second He is present under the Species of bread and wine that signify His Body and Blood.

The Church venerates both Presences of Christ: "The Church has always venerated the divine Scriptures as she venerates the Body of the Lord, since from the table of both the Word of God and the Body of Christ she unceasingly receives and offers to the faithful the Bread of Life."[25]

In both cases, Christ becomes present for us to help us become new human beings. Then when we become transformed, we will be able to transform others and eventually the whole world.

In the Liturgy of the Word, we listen to Jesus Who speaks His Word to us *today*. We must respond to Him with the Responsorial Psalm. Then we have that Word made actual for us in the Homily which is the incarnation of Christ's Word in our day. In the Creed we accept that actualization and in the Prayer of the Faithful we express our community's personal response to the Word by applying it to various life-situations that affect our parish and the whole world.

In the Liturgy of the Eucharist, Christ comes to us under the visible signs of bread and wine. He anticipates for the Church the transforming effect of the Resurrection. In a veiled and partial way He transforms the world into what it will be at the end of time.

Jesus thereby gives Himself *in Person* to the Church. He makes the truth of His Resurrection valid for each of us by His power. He is given to us in the things of the world, which He invisibly transforms into the Body of His Resurrection.

The Eucharist thus becomes the vehicle by which the world is no longer solely the place where human beings live out their lives on the material level, but the place where Christ comes to us daily in the Spirit. It is the vehicle which effects a transformation in Christians and in the world which is wrought by the Risen Christ.

Our encounter with Christ's Presence in the Eucharist through Communion must, however, contribute to this transformation. We must accept the daily effort for justice and love in our lives and those of others. We must break down the barriers of selfishness and become true children of God.

Only by being transformed into Christ can we hope to transform the world into His Body and thus pave the way for the final victory of Christ over sin and evil.

In concluding it might be well to point out that each of the three Eucharistic aspects mentioned above has an objective reality and each calls for a subjective response on the part of those who participate in the Eucharist.

The Eucharist re-enacts Christ's Sacrifice and applies its merits to us in time. But it also calls for a sacrifice of praise on our part and a spiritual offering of our own in union with Christ.

The Eucharist commemorates the Covenant of God with His people in the History of Salvation and makes that history present for us today. At the same time it summons us to ratify God's wondrous Covenant with us by entering deeply into the Divine Plan of Salvation.

The Eucharist brings Christ present before us in an invisible but completely real manner that transforms the world. We must work with Christ's Presence so that we will be transformed into "other Christs," new human beings.

If we participate completely in every Eucharist we will receive the Divine benefits found in it and be able to apply it to our lives as well as to the world around us. We will be doing our bit to transform the world for Christ in preparation for His Second Coming in glory.

Chapter 5
# WHATEVER HAPPENED TO THE COMMENTATOR?

Some fifteen years ago in the first flush of enthusiasm for the liturgical reforms of Vatican II, one of the names most bandied about was that of *commentator*. He seemed to do everything but actually celebrate Mass.

It was the *commentator* who insured continuity for and understanding of the rite, connected disparate parts, introduced the Readings, and in general saw to it that everything was in order. He was patterned after the on-the-air commentators who made television Masses understandable to mixed audiences all over the world.

The commentator functioned as a kind of master of ceremonies who provided the link between celebrant and people. As such, his contribution was invaluable.

In due time, the office of commentator was even made a proper liturgical one and the new *Sacramentary* of 1974 speaks (in a section on "Special Ministers") specifically about that role and its purpose:

> The commentator gives explanations and directives to the people; he introduces the celebration and helps the people to understand it better. His comments should be carefully prepared, clear, and succinct.[26]

The obvious conclusion to all this is that the commentator is a position of no little import. The Liturgy is a community action of a hierarchical nature—that is, all the faithful, both clergy and laity, have an active role in virtue of the Sacrament of Baptism. *It is the function of the commentator to coordinate these active roles.*

Accordingly, commentators must have a complete knowledge of the Liturgy which comes only from long association and careful training. They must also be completely reliable and ever punctual. They are a *must* for any celebration.

## A Vanishing Breed

Yet the plain fact is that in the years that have followed the initial euphoria, the commentator has become a vanishing breed. Even renowned Liturgists have mentioned the office only grudgingly and rushed to place restrictions on it.

What are the reasons given for this about-face? And do they hold up? One reason given implicitly is that *there is no longer any need for a commentator since everybody knows what to do at Mass by now!* In such circumstances the commentator becomes something of a superfluity. He clutters the rite needlessly with verbiage and becomes a distraction rather than an aid.

This objection would be true enough in some idealistic community where all the members were thoroughly familiar with their Faith and their worship. However, it is an oversimplification in the real world of most Catholics. It simply does not jibe with the facts.

Most services without a commentator (or anyone who assumes his function) become rag-tag affairs that do harm to the beauty of the Liturgy and prevent the people from participating to their fullest ability in the Liturgy.

Another reason is that there is *no need for the role of the commentator* because the celebrant actually carries it out. Once again this is only a partial truth. Yes, some celebrants with a charismatic personality do act as their own commentators and keep their actions flowing without distraction or interruption.

However, there is a harmful side effect from such a procedure. The celebrant usurps another's role in the Liturgy. In the history of the Liturgy no good has resulted from such usurpings, no matter how well intentioned. That is why the Second Vatican Council went to great lengths to insure that in the Liturgy everyone should do his/her part and only that part:

> In liturgical celebrations, whether as a minister or as one of the faithful, each person should perform his role by doing solely and totally what the nature of things and liturgical norms require of him.[27]

By departing from this essential norm in the present case, the celebrant is kept so busy that he inevitably interferes with the performance of the role that is his—to appear as a detached yet involved president of the assembly, functioning both as intermediary for and as part of the people. Unquestionably, one or other of the characteristics of his priestly role will be blurred or lost completely in the eyes of the people.

## Whatever Happened to the Commentator?    45

I recently had occasion to attend a Bar Mitzvah. The service was beautiful and well done. The rabbi was excellent, an adroit leader and considerate master of ceremonies—presenting, interpreting, guiding, and commenting.

However, one thing was wrong. The rabbi took all the parts. He dominated the whole performance. After a while you thought of him as a master of ceremonies. This little nuance can take much away from any celebration. It throws the perspective off and does much harm in a subtle way. At the very least, it diminishes the position of the leader. It is as if the President of the United States were to speak on television and act as his own announcer!

The same fate overtakes the dynamic celebrant who takes over the part of the commentator. The people may come to identify with him more as a commentator than as their leader who represents Christ.

Moreover, in many places the celebrant can't assume the role of the commentator. It is taxing, time-consuming, confusing, and takes him away from doing his part. *So he omits it!*

A third reason alleged for the lack of a commentator is that *"no one is capable of doing it."* The requirements are beyond most members of our congregations. Who has a good grasp of Liturgy, a good voice, and time to devote to this task? It is difficult to find people with that kind of expertise, but it is not impossible.

Religious (brothers or sisters) immediately come to mind. Then there are members of the Liturgy Committee who can provide instruction and training for them. Finally, there are the readers. Perhaps some of them could alternate as readers and as commentators from week to week.

As an extreme measure, the leader of song or the reader could double as a commentator at the same celebration. This is a usurpation of roles but less harmful than when the celebrant does it.

### Need for Commentator

The sad fact is that without a commentator the Liturgy is missing a very important part for the people. We must realize that, contrary to what we may want to believe, the average person in the pew has very little understanding of the Eucharist as it is. Without help, that person will not benefit from the new Liturgy to the extent that the Church intends and will completely lose the teaching value of the sacred action.

The first aspect of the Liturgy—worship of God and sanctification of one's person—can be obtained. But it will be obtained in fuller fashion with a commentator who makes insightful comments at key parts of the service. But the second aspect of the Liturgy which was stressed by Vatican II will be harder to obtain:

> Although the Sacred Liturgy is above all things the worship of the divine Majesty, it likewise contains abundant instruction for the faithful. For in the Liturgy God speaks to His people and Christ is still proclaiming His Gospel. And the people reply to God both by song and by prayer.[28]

The Liturgy is the one time when the community comes together in the normal course of things. It is perfect for instruction in the Faith. The Homily can give part of this instruction. But the whole ceremony is filled with instructions for us—the gestures, prayers, songs, symbols, readings, and the rites within rites are all vehicles of instruction. The Liturgy is a veritable *school of the Faith*, if only we use it.

For example, how can the average worshiper know what liturgical mood to take on any given Sunday if no comment is made about the season at the beginning of Mass? "What?" you will answer, "how can any Catholic not know the liturgical season?" Not all Catholics live the Liturgy to the hilt.

Those Catholics who do not live by the liturgical seasons in no way feel guilty about this lack. They feel that they go to church precisely to find out about religious (that is, liturgical) things. Faced with such an attitude, we must be determined to utilize the Liturgy to inform our people and help them celebrate the Eucharist as fully as possible for them. Thus, a good introduction means a great deal.

Then there are the Readings—excerpts from books written centuries ago, many of them completely unfamiliar to the average Catholic. In such circumstances, the simple reading of the text means relatively little without some background. A judicious introductory word will work wonders, getting people into the flow of the passage and enabling them to understand the word God is speaking to them through that Reading.

The people will then be able to respond more genuinely and knowledgeably to that Word. They will be more open to it because they will be participating more consciously in the proclamation of the Word of God.

Before the Eucharistic Prayer the commentator can do a great service for the congregation. He can announce which prayer is being used by the celebrant and briefly indicate its main theme. From time to time he can also

## Whatever Happened to the Commentator? 47

call attention to one of its major parts, recalling the sentiments that should be theirs during the most important part of the Mass.

At the end of the Eucharistic Prayer, the commentator can get the congregation ready to give their full assent to what has taken place and to confirm their offering of self with Christ. He can remind them that they have offered themselves with Christ to the Father and will now prepare to receive Him from the Father as their supernatural nourishment.

### Helps Mold Worshipers into a Community

Perhaps the most important role of the commentator is that he helps mold the worshipers into a community. He insures that they will not be present simply as individuals but as parts of a worshiping community. Even in specialized audiences when the commentator's interventions are not necessary for the purpose of imparting instruction, they are very useful in rallying the attention of the people and fostering their sense of unity.

The primary requisite for liturgical prayer in the fullest sense is to have a real community. For the Liturgy itself is "the worship which the community of Christ's faithful pays to the Eternal Father."[29] Now the simple juxtaposition of individuals who happen to have chosen the same time and place to fulfill a personal obligation does not of itself constitute them into a community.

They must become explicitly aware of their unity. They must become conscious that they form a society, a family, a church. Use of a Missal or Missalette will help them personally but will not necessarily weld them into a community.

If a commentator addresses each directly and makes common exhortations, they will become one, an audience. People at a public event such as a play or a ball game will spontaneously rise as one to applaud a bravura performance or an outstanding physical feat, because they know what the play or the game is all about.

On the other hand, when an unknown fact is announced, the people do not respond as one. They react to it merely as individuals. But if the fact is placed within the perspective of the event they are participating in, they react spontaneously and in unison. They become a community once again, a community held together by the event. Strangers smile and nod knowingly to one another in the flush of their enthusiasm and their on-the-spot unity.

It is this type of enthusiasm that a commentator can engender at a Eucharistic Celebration. The celebrant cannot because it would be out of place. The commentator can elicit interest because that is precisely his role—to comment, instruct, and direct. Thus, he will more easily bring about a participation on the part of the people that is full, active, and conscious in accord with the fervent desire of the Church.

In recent years more and more Catholics have voiced the lament that the Mystery of the Mass has been lost for them. They bemoan the lack of silence, the constant singing, the banal appearance of the entire rite. Since one of the greatest components of mystery is *inaccessibility*, could they really be saying that the celebrant is too *accessible* to the Congregation?

Once he was far removed from the people—totally apart from them by the design of the churches, silent prayer, and a foreign tongue. Now he celebrates in their very midst, in full voice, and in their own tongue—and most find this beautiful. However, such accessibility can lead to loss of mystery. It can blur the distinction between priest and people and make their parts the same from one point of view. Perhaps a commentator placed between priest and people might hint at the tremendous mystery involved.

The commentator should foster community worship, and should draw the people into the liturgical action rather than set them off into independent action. We need commentators who do not call attention to themselves and their words but to the celebrant and his words. They are not lecturers giving a class but links between celebrant and people. They are not preachers engaged in moralizing or reporters concerned with describing but "precursors" who must lead the people to the celebrant who will in turn bind them fast to Christ.

Such a role is demanding and it will not be easily attained. Until we get genuine commentators functioning at Mass we are only kidding ourselves about the value of the new Liturgy and all the good that the people are receiving. Religious culture is on the wane in our day and liturgical understanding is very low among people.

Recently a Liturgy committee member mentioned that she had been approached by a woman who liked the new altar of her church but was perplexed as to why the word "ow" had to be on the cloth that covered it. Christ did suffer but was it necessary to keep that word there! The word in question was of course the symbol of Christ made up of the letters "alpha" and "omega" of the Greek alphabet. As the first and last letters of that alphabet, they have always been applied by the Church to Jesus, the beginning and the end of all things—the Lord of Lords.

Unless a person knows this fact, the symbolism—beautiful though it is—will be completely lost and perhaps engender erroneous suppositions as in the case mentioned.

The long-range answer to such religious ignorance is catechesis, which is another problem. But the short-range answer may well be the use of a competent commentator at Mass. At least he will insure one thing—that all in his audience will have access to the minimal liturgical culture needed by every Catholic in order to participate fully, consciously, and actively at the single most important action of Catholic life.

Chapter 6
# LITURGY AND CREATIVITY

In the wake of the Second Vatican Council, the Liturgy of the Church became big news—carried by the newspapers, discussed in periodicals, and dissected in a host of books. As the Church began the exciting and gigantic task of reforming all the liturgical rites and issuing a new set of liturgical books, it became the thing to speak and write about Liturgy.

As time went on interest began to wane—even before all the reforms were completed. All the major rites were completed and some were taken for granted. The Liturgy was no longer news.

Of course in the eyes of the Church the Liturgy had never lost its luster. After all it is the supreme rite of the Liturgy, the *Eucharist*, which "makes the Church" and the Church which "makes the Eucharist"—as Pope John Paul II has reiterated only recently.

Thus the Church bided its time while many of the faithful went off into other areas and paid scant attention to the Liturgy. Then at a propitious moment the Church made Liturgy become news once again. Pope John Paul issued a masterly letter on Liturgy during Lent of 1980 and it made headlines even in the secular press, although it was very much misrepresented.

Then on April 30 of the same year the Sacred Congregation for the Sacraments and Divine Worship followed with an *Instruction concerning Worship of the Eucharistic Mystery* that was immediately labeled "reactionary" by the secular press. *The New York Times*, for example, in a flagrant display of biased reporting went so far as to place a photo of the Traditionalist Archbishop Lefebvre next to its front-page story about this instruction. The reader thus received the clear impression that the Pope was coming round to the renegade Archbishop's position on the Liturgy. As many Catholic papers pointed out, such was definitely not the case.

Nevertheless, a feeling has remained in the air that creativity in Liturgy is being curbed or the Pope is in the process of taking away some of the liturgical gains won at the Second Vatican Council.

Not one of the liturgical gains has been taken away. *Nothing has been curbed except false creativity or to put it another way liturgical license,* that is, the distortion of the legitimate creativity granted by the Church to all who participate in its Liturgy. This point is brought home most effectively by the ideas contained in an article printed in the liturgical organ of the Church, *Notitiae* for April of 1980. The author is Father Adrian Nocent, one of the world-ranking liturgists, and it was first given as a speech at the first National Liturgical Conference held in Senegal (in May 1979).

### The Liturgy as "Moment" of Salvation

The Liturgy is for us the "now" of a historical event, which is situated in a specific time and place but at the same time escapes all time and place in being rendered present for us. "When we celebrate the mysteries of the Lord, we do not celebrate them as past events but as events taking place today before our eyes" (St. Leo the Great).

These mysteries are celebrated through the mediation of sacred signs, for it remains true that no one in this world can see God face to face. We can discern supernatural realities only in conformity with our actual nature and according to our proper manner of knowing, which faith elevates but never suppresses. Just as the communication of thoughts presupposes the mediation of the sensible between our spirits, so the communication of supernatural realities presupposes both human nature and history.

Those who want to take part in a supernatural event must—like all who take part in any natural event—obey the laws of the event in question. For example, those who came to see and hear Christ preach during His life on earth had to use their eyes to see and their ears to hear—but they could not see or hear Him if they went to the mountains instead of the seashore where He was preaching. The event of seeing and hearing Christ in the flesh had its own rules, and all who wanted to experience it had to obey them.

In the event that they did encounter Christ physically, they could not understand what He said unless they knew Aramaic, the earthly language that He spoke. That was part of the "ritual" of Christ's life as it drew itself, out, and it had its own rules. Such rules are ingrained in events by the Creator by the simple act of having created things the way they are, and all who want to participate in events must conform to them.

Liturgy and Creativity 53

In the saving events which are made present again for us today, the Church has laid down certain rules for participants which flow for the most part from the nature of these events. They insure that the events may be rightly performed and rendered truly actual. These are their *rites*. To take genuine part in such saving events that make Christ present, and to take full advantage of the salvation He brings us, we must "obey" the rules at any given moment.

### The Liturgy as "Memorial" of the Mysteries of Salvation

Vatican II has sometimes been accused of eliminating the Real Presence of Christ in the "new Liturgy" by the use of the word "Memorial." Such an accusation takes no account of the fact that "Memorial" presupposes the *reality of presence*.

We "remind" God of what He has done for His people, and in order to do so we render the *past actual* to the eye of God, so to speak. Whenever God is reminded, it is always a *new activity*; and it is at this moment that we ask Him for something. The Psalms often utilize this type of "memorial."

Thus, when Jesus says: "Do this in memory of Me," he does not signify merely that the sacrificial banquet of the Last Supper and the Mass will recall Him to the memory of His disciples and of people who will follow them throughout the ages. He means: "celebrate this sacrificial banquet, which presents My sacrifice that has established the new and eternal Covenant."

Every liturgical celebration finds its meaning therein: making present Christ, and the events of the Old Testament that He unites in Himself, in the present, for the future: the reconstruction of the world and the end of time.

### The Real Presence of the Lord and His Mysteries

Vatican II rectified a situation in which Catholics were accustomed to seeing Christ's presence only in the Eucharist. It did so in its *Constitution on the Sacred Liturgy* by delineating the various presences of Christ in the Liturgy:

> Christ is always present in His Church, especially in her liturgical celebrations. He is present in the sacrifice of the Mass, not only in the presence of His minister, . . . but especially under the Eucharistic species. By His power He is present in the sacraments so that when

a man baptizes, it is really Christ Himself who baptizes. He is present in His Word, since it is He Himself who speaks when the Holy Scriptures are read in the Church. He is present, lastly, when the Church prays and sings, for He promised: "Where two or three are gathered together in My Name, there am I in the midst of them" (Mt 18:20).[30]

However, Vatican II did not provide a sufficient theology of what we must understand by this presence of the Lord in these different modes. Is there a real presence only in the Mass? And in the other modes is there an analogous presence, a simple assistance on the part of the Lord?

The opposite view risks lumping all of the modes together and seeing an identical mode in the proclamation of the Lord, for example, and in the Eucharist. Another view confines the Lord's presence solely to the Eucharist.

This last view is unfortunately the one held by most Catholics. They stroll into church during the proclamation of the Word of God and even go to confession during the proclamation of the Scriptures. Priests abstain from speaking in the Homily about what the Lord has said but touch on everything else. Such actions are graphic illustrations of the lack of conviction of a real presence of the Lord during these parts of Mass.

In the *Encyclical On the Mystery of Faith*, Paul VI insists strongly on the real Eucharistic Presence and our faith in it. He states: "When I call the Eucharistic Presence *real* I mean real not by excluding the reality of the other modes of Christ's presence but I mean real *par excellence!*"[31]

What does the Pope mean by this? When a person baptizes, the water remains water and after the celebration of baptism there is no longer any presence of Christ! When a reader proclaims the Word of God during a Liturgy of the Word, the book remains what it is and after the proclamation there is no longer any presence of Christ.

However, when a priest celebrates the Eucharist, the bread is no longer bread and the wine is no longer wine; and for the length of time that the sacramental signs perdure the Real Presence of Christ perdures. Hence, it is not the presence itself that loses its reality as in the other modes of Christ's presence; rather it is the mode according to which the reality of this presence is achieved that is different.

### Need for True Creativity

It is evident that we have a great need for true creativity in the Liturgy—a creativity that gives full value to every rite, word, and gesture. This is a *first creativity* or *creativity par excellence* and it consists in re-creating what we have received, in realizing that we are going to bring about an event in what we celebrate—a saving event. As such, this obligation falls upon all who participate in liturgical celebrations, and especially the one who presides and his ministers.

They must make it their business to re-create the text to be proclaimed, just as a musician re-creates a work that his audience knows by heart, that he himself has played so many times previously, and yet enchants all who hear it anew.

This is also true of the Eucharistic Prayer. The priest's rendition of it will hold the attention of his audience and usher them into the saving event of Christ's passion, death, and resurrection, not only when he carries it out meticulously and completely but also and above all when he has taken pains to study it, commit it to memory, and pray it often. Only when each Eucharistic Prayer has truly become his, will he be able to make it become part of every person in the assembly.

Creativity must extend to the lives of all who participate in the Liturgy. There is no real Liturgy without the sanctification of people. When we designate the Liturgy as "moment" we must understand what we mean by it. It presupposes a *continuity of life*.

Each of us has our own personal altar on which we offer continually in a sacrifice of praise and petition to the Father. But this activity bursts forth and reaches its peak at the moment of the liturgical celebration, when each person brings his or her personal altar to the main altar, in the presence of God's majesty, offering with Christ and being offered in his offering.

Every Liturgy presupposes such a continuity of life, and there is no true celebration unless we bring it into our concrete lives and make efforts to carry out the will of the Father. The conclusion of each liturgical celebration should find us on a higher level than its beginning and looking forward to the start of the next celebration on our journey to the Father.

On leaving the celebration, what could we think of except what the Lord has said and done? Our whole life will thus be centered on the liturgical activity-contemplation.

A liturgical spirituality is *the* spirituality for all of us. There are many spiritualities in the Church—those of St. Francis and St. Ignatius, for example, and we are free to follow any one of them. But we always have the Liturgy as a spirituality that figures in all others.

We can have special devotion to the Blessed Mother or to St. Francis—and that is fine, but we must take account of a hierarchy of values. The primary spirituality is that of the Liturgy, and it must show in our manner of celebrating it and living it in our lives. If we celebrate the month of May in honor of Mary, for example, we can do so in such a way that it will not take away from the themes of the Easter Season in which May usually falls. We will then not only be giving honor to Mary, but doing so in a way that demonstrates her true role in the history of salvation and what it means to us today.

It is this type of creativity that is of paramount importance for us today. Yet it is precisely such creativity that is ignored. We are simply re-creating something that was there all along.

I believe it is this very type of creativity that the Church wants all of us to pursue. For if we re-create the Liturgy in this way, we will attain a true liturgical spirituality. And such a solid base will then enable all to add on whatever type of spirituality they prefer with no fear of going astray.

Chapter 7
# LITURGICAL SPIRITUALITY

In the Mass we have God-with-Us (Emmanuel), the Lord Jesus among us. It seems to me that Catholics fail to make much of this point in their lives. They fail to realize the wondrous spirituality that is at our fingertips in the Liturgy (the Mass, the Sacraments, and the Liturgy of the Hours).

We take all this for granted, yet it is very real. The Mass combines God's transcendence and His immanence in a marvelous manner. In the Liturgy of the Word the accent is on transcendence (although immanence is not lacking) and in the Liturgy of the Eucharist the spotlight is on immanence (although transcendence is not absent).

Thus, we have available a complete spirituality in the Liturgy, especially in the Mass. The sole problem is how to make good use of it.

One of the tragedies of the present day is that Catholics go running after all kinds of spiritualities—Eastern, psychological, practical—and unknowingly discard the most powerful spirituality in their own backyard, so to speak. They remain oblivious of the Eucharistic spirituality that is waiting for them in their parish churches.

One of the reasons for this anomaly is that Catholics have lost the one vehicle that imparted such a spirituality—the popular Missal. The sole means at their disposal for imbibing this genuine spirituality of the Church is by participating during the Mass itself.

Unfortunately this is not enough for the vast majority of them. It does not suffice for them to obtain a spirituality that will permeate their lives away from the church. Most Catholics can be likened in this respect to the person mentioned by St. James who looks in the mirror but then goes away from it and forgets what he or she looks like (Jm 1:23-24).

They resemble the Jews led out of Egypt by Moses who pined for the fleshpots of Egypt, although they had the living God with them in the desert.

Hence, Catholics who would participate one hundred percent in the

Liturgy of the Mass would undoubtedly be capable of practicing a genuine Eucharistic spirituality in their lives. Such a full participation is difficult to attain. It requires great intelligence, complete emotional control, total openness to experience, and the highest powers of assimilation, retention, and meditation.

For those who do not possess such sublime powers of the spirit, the riches of Eucharistic spirituality can only become part of their lives through the riches found in a personal Missal.

**Forerunners and Advent of the People's Missal**

From the start of the Church, the Eucharist has been the center of Christian life. All understood that participation in the Eucharistic Celebration is in itself source and end of the spiritual life, for it is in the Eucharist that the faithful become one with Christ.

Hence, many attempts have been made over the centuries to render the Mystery of the Eucharist more comprehensible in its unfolding through the Liturgical Year. In this way, the Church might inculcate in her members an even deeper penetration into the peace and strength as well as enrichment of life that can be derived from the Eucharist.

We might recall the mystagogical explanations of the Eucharist on the part of the Fathers, the early commentaries on the Mass, or the "Mass explanations" of the Carolingian days. Added to these are the twofold type of Mass literature of the Middle Ages: the theological treatises and the allegorical explanations.

Finally, when the Mass texts were collected into one source—the Roman Missal of Pius V—the beginnings of the popular Missal for the people began to issue forth. These were originally made up of extracts from the Missal with explanations, since the Canon could not be printed in popular books. Eventually, they became full-scale translations of the book at the altar.

With the advent of the twentieth century, the people's Missal flourished. It was the Missal which made the Latin Liturgy understandable by the people in depth. And it was the Missal which brought about popular participation on the part of the assembly.

This was true in spite of the fact that participation was hindered by (1) the non-vernacular language of the Liturgy, (2) the failure of the Tridentine Liturgy to be structured for participation by the assembly, and (3) the accent on the Liturgy as a preserve of the clergy.

Thus, a genuine spirituality of the Liturgical Year came into being, aided immensely by the impetus of the Liturgical Movement and the Biblical Renewal. The Missal had become a wonderful instrument for Eucharistic spirituality.

Unfortunately, this upward movement toward a Missal-inspired-spirituality came to an abrupt end with the renewed Liturgy of Vatican II.

It was in no way intended by the Council Fathers. Neither is there any real reason for it. Yet the sad fact is that the popular Missal has been relegated to oblivion because of the New Liturgy.

The reasons are many but the most effective one revolves around the fact that since the Liturgy is now in the vernacular, everyone feels that he or she knows all there is to know about the Mass. This puts Catholics in the position of those who believe they understand a subject simply because they know the words spoken.

Hence, there is the growing complaint on all sides that people "get nothing out of the Mass." Without the aid of a Missal it is all too true that the real spirituality of the Liturgy will escape them.

### The Missal—Best Instrument of Eucharistic Spirituality

The sole purpose of the Liturgy is to make us enter into the Mystery of God's presence in Jesus Christ. The Eucharist is in the first place a Mystery of Salvation by God which is accomplished in human beings. Through this sacred rite, Jesus Christ comes to the faithful, takes up His abode with them, and desires to make them His temple, His Body.

The Liturgy is intended to assist believers in opening themselves to the presence of God in Jesus Christ in this Sacrament of His Church and to include their voices in the choir of the Church both on earth and in heaven.

If we are to profit spiritually from the ineffable riches of the Liturgy we must *know it, love it, and live it*. The best way to do this is by participating in it *fully, consciously, and actively*.

Such a participation will make us so involved in the Eucharist (*know* it) that it will become part of our person (*loved* by us) and its effects will spill over into our everyday lives (*lived* by us). The Missal is invaluable for inculcating these attitudes in us.

The Missal gives us a knowledge of the Mystery of Faith. It is a textbook of the teachings of the Faith, but it is not a dry series of propositions. The teaching pervades every page and every action that it describes, it being a living instrument of knowledge.

This same book gives us a prayerbook of our own. It teaches us to pray with the "mind of the Church," and thus eliminates the dangers of self-centered prayers. It introduces us to the Bible and provides us with the Church's commentary on that Word of God, and provides a wonderful introduction into the Eucharist and its place in the Sacramental Order. A diligent use of the Missal will give a liturgical culture beyond any other book.

### The Missal—A Book of General Initiation into the Faith

The Liturgy is the living expression of the Church's *deposit of Faith*. Thus, the Missal is the living Catechism of the Catholic Religion. It is the written testimony of what the Church prays, believes, and proclaims.

The Missal does not present the Faith in a way that follows life, so to speak. It enables people to come in contact with the Faith in a manner that helps them make it part of their lives.

Those who enter into the spirit of the Liturgy as presented in the Missal acquire a genuine Liturgical Culture. This enables them to become incorporated into the Faith of the Church as expressed in its unfolding of the Mystery of Salvation throughout the Liturgical Year.

The Mystery of Salvation accomplished by Jesus in the unity of the Spirit and in accord with the design of the Father is inexhaustible. With each participation in the Liturgy, Catholics who use the Missal to full advantage and participate to their utmost gain a deeper understanding of that Mystery. They also grow in love for it and apply it more effectively in their daily lives.

We are so fortunate that we can obtain a greater knowledge of our Faith while praying the Liturgy. While doing something beneficial to our salvation and the salvation of the world, we are also learning what it means, a wonderful benefit through the use of a Missal.

### The Missal—Prayer Book of the Church

The Liturgy is a veritable "school of prayer" and the Missal is the Church's basic prayer book, an initiation into Christian prayer. The Missal teaches us *how to pray*. It shows us that every prayer should be one of *praise, thanksgiving, and petition*. Every petition is to be preceded by rendering thanks to God for His past and present favors.

Every true prayer is *Trinitarian*—and the Missal clearly brings this home to us. It is the Spirit who suggests the words to us, Jesus who offers our prayer, and the Father who accepts it. We must pray always in this vein.

The Missal teaches us to avoid particularism, self-centeredness, and one-sidedness. Our personal prayer is seen in perspective with the lives of our co-parishioners, co-members of the Church, and co-members of the human race. We never pray alone—just as we never live alone in this world. What we do always touches others in one way or another.

The Missal *provides content* for our prayer. It contains over 2,000 prayers on many subjects, which are based on the language and spirit of the Word of God in the Bible. It enables us to pray *with the Church* by giving us model prayers to use in many life situations. Many consider them to have been inspired by the Holy Spirit.

This entire treasury of liturgical prayers is pervaded by the Bible. It constitutes an inexhaustible source of genuine piety for all Christians.

The Missal teaches us *when to pray*—always. The Eucharist can be celebrated in conjunction with the Liturgy of the Hours or Divine Office— which is the official prayer book of the Church. Thus, the Missal shows that the whole of life is a kind of public service for God, one long prayer—the prayer of the hours.

We can tune in to this prayer by uniting with the *prayers themselves* or by utilizing *invocations* that are also available in the Missal: "Lord, have mercy," "Thanks be to God," etc. No matter how we use it, the Missal gives us a truly Christian prayer—a way of praying to God in spirit and in truth.

### The Missal—A Book of Biblical Initiation

During every Eucharistic celebration, the Word of God is proclaimed, pondered, and made effectual. We listen to it and the listening becomes a prayer that makes the Word relevant to our day. The Church reads from the Bible, prays with the Bible, worships God's Word in the Liturgy, and lives on that Word.

Our Liturgy is almost entirely fashioned out of the Word of God. As a matter of fact, the Liturgy is sometimes termed "the Bible in Action. "For it includes Readings which are *taken* from the Bible; antiphons which are *adapted* from the Bible; songs which *reflect* the Bible; greetings, acclamations, and institution narrative which are *based* on the Bible; Prayers which are *inspired* by the Bible; the Homily which *explains* the Bible.

The Church is well aware that she was formed by the Bible and that the

Bible was written with worship in mind. The Bible continues to form God's people today—especially through the Liturgy, and in particular the Eucharist. As the theological maxim puts it, "The Eucharist makes the Church."

At the same time, the Word of God can be truly understood in the Liturgy. The latter offers the true background for the proper interpretation of God's Word.

The Missal coordinates Word and Sacrament—in the living practice of the Church. The Word of God becomes proclamation and salvation. The book, which is dead in itself, comes to life for when it is *spoken* in a context of faith, it inculcates faith, and it increases faith.

### The Missal—A Book of Liturgical Initiation

The Missal is a service book for the Eucharistic celebration. It contains the rites and prayers by which the *Paschal Mystery of Christ's Death and Resurrection* is made present in the religious worship of the People of God *in assembly*. The Missal acquaints everyone with the manner in which the Church celebrates the Liturgy and brings about the Lord's liturgical Presence. Just as the best way to discover prayer is to practice it, so the best way to understand the Liturgy is to participate fully in it.

The Missal also contains the rites and prayers for the sacraments. It thus places them in the proper perspective for those who make use of the Missal. It shows the true relationship of all the sacraments to the Eucharistic Sacrifice and to each other.

The Missal helps people to participate in all aspects of the Liturgy and thus becomes the most effective book for liturgical initiation. The texts and rubrics or directions bring out the essence of worship in an existential way. They express what human language and signs offer to God in praise and thanksgiving and they proclaim God's saving acts in the past, the present, and the future.

The Missal aids participation by presenting the people with the opportunity to meditate on the liturgical texts before the Eucharist and to go over them afterward. It provides at least a minimum knowledge of what is taking place in the Liturgy. It can be a springboard to attaining a complete knowledge of the Liturgy and a genuine love for it.

The watchword of those who used Missals in their heyday was: "Follow the Mass with a Missal." With this in mind, people are beginning to fashion a new watchword out of it. "You don't need a Missal to follow the Mass any more. You need a Missal to make the Mass follow you home and in your daily life."

### The Missal—The Catholic's Book Par Excellence

It is clear that the spirituality needed by Catholics today is a Eucharistic one. It is equally clear that the Missal is the best instrument for the attainment of such a spirituality.

The Missal should be *the* book for every Catholic. Many of us take it for granted. What would we do if we did not have one available! We would be without the single book that gives the essence of our Eucharist, which is in turn the essence of our religious and secular existence. Under such circumstances, I dare say that even the Bible *by itself* could not satisfy us.

The one thing we do not want to do is to give up such a treasure out of a lack of realization of what it really is. The Missal is our sure guide to a Eucharistic spirituality, which is our ticket to a real Christian life.

Chapter 8
# THE ROLE OF SILENCE IN LITURGICAL CELEBRATIONS

We live in an age of almost uninterrupted communication or sound. We are bombarded with stimuli coming in to us from the outside through our senses: sounds, sights, and smells as well as touches and tastes.

This continuous stream of impressions that invades our person is the lifestyle that we live with. We adapt to it and we somehow function in spite of it. Yet there is also the need for silence—time to concentrate on our relationship to God, time to get close to God, time to see ourselves from the outside, so to speak.

It is true that we can find God in the midst of noise and confusion. Especially when we use the eyes of faith, we can see His hand all around us—even in the very frenetic pace with which our lives are carried forward. It is difficult but it can be done.

Yet it is also true that an attitude of "faith, hope, and love for God, which is open to the gift of the Spirit, and also a brotherly love, which is open to the mystery of others, carry with them an imperative need for silence."[32]

By silence we mean—to use once more the words of Paul VI[33]—a pause amid all the noises, all the impressions of the senses, all the voices, which the environment compels us to listen to, making us turn outward, deafening us, while it fills us with echoes, images, stimuli, which—whether we like it or not—paralyze our inner freedom to think and pray.

Silence does not mean sleep; it means a talk with ourselves, quiet reflection, an act of conscience, a moment of personal solitude, an attempt to recuperate ourselves.

Such silence has the capacity of listening. Listening to what? To whom? We cannot say; but we know that spiritual listening allows us—if God grants us the grace—to hear His voice, that voice of His which is immediately distinguished by sweetness and strength and the Word of God.

## Liturgical Silence

Accordingly, the Church has included a *liturgical silence* at various places in the new rites, especially the Eucharistic celebration. Such silence is not intended to reduce the faithful to participating in the liturgical action like strangers and mute spectators. Rather its purpose is to insert the people more deeply into the mystery being celebrated.

The faithful can never again be given such a nonparticipant role, for by rebirth and the anointing of the Holy Spirit they have been consecrated into a royal priesthood. Although this common priesthood of the faithful differs from the ministerial priesthood in essence as well as in degree, it still requires that the faithful take a real part in the sacred action of the Liturgy—which can be done even through a fruitful silence.

Liturgical silence attains its goal by means of the inner dispositions which flow from the Word of God that is listened to, the chants and prayers that are voiced, and the spiritual union with the celebrant in the parts that are his alone.

By this religious silence, which is now an integral part of the sacred action, the faithful (1) reenter within themselves, (2) reflect briefly on what they have heard, or (3) praise God and pray to Him in the depths of their spirit.

So highly does the Church value this liturgical silence that she has even written rubrical directions into all the new rites. The new edition of the *Roman Missal* has such directions both in the *Lectionary* and in the *Sacramentary*. Moreover, the American edition of the *Sacramentary* has specifically alluded to these rubrics in a special Foreword.

The character of each specific moment of liturgical silence depends on the time when it occurs in the particular celebration. But it is the celebrant who orchestrates it for his community.

He can do this by his own bearing which is one of genuine recollection yet not distant abstraction. He is present amid the people as their leader in prayer but also as their brother wayfarer who shares their trials as well as their joys. He presents them with a demeanor to follow.

More than this, however, he should also encourage the people at suitable points in the celebration to use the liturgical silence well. He clearly but briefly points out what is the reason for the silence in question and what they should be doing at the moment.

Without such coaching, the majority of people in the assembly will simply dissipate the silence and gain no benefit from it whatever. They just will not know what to do with it. Hence, it is of paramount importance that the celebrant help them with his words—even though he may think he is repeating himself over and over. In this matter there is no such thing as too much catechizing.

### 1. Silence—for Self-examination

At the Penitential Rite during Mass, a judicious word of the celebrant may move the assembly to make a brief but realistic examination of conduct toward God, Church, and others (especially those of the community and assembly).

Thus the people may be led to reflect that their community and the present assembly as a whole should be open to God on beginning this most august rite of the Eucharist.

With the Sign of Peace in mind, they may go further and become reconciled with their neighbor who had offended them or whom they had offended. In this way they will be carrying out Christ's injunction to be reconciled to one another before offering their sacrifice.

This part of the rite will then become for the people a true sacramental that forgives their venial faults and readies them for union with Jesus.

### 2. Silence—for Formulating Petitions

Again, at the Opening Prayer a careful remark by the celebrant—such as, "Let us reflect for a moment that we are petitioning God in the name of Christ and His Church and add our intentions silently"—will enlighten the people about the silence at this point and help them make the most of it.

Failure to include this word, or even to provide time for a liturgical silence here, takes much away from the prayer that the celebrant utters. For in this particular prayer the celebrant is the interpreter of a great number of diverse needs of each individual who participates at that Mass. He invites the faithful to exercise their general priesthood by prayer ("Let us pray" is not meant to be an empty formula). Indeed, his role is to gather and express them in the official prayer of the day.

However, the people need to formulate their intentions or petitions. They bring to this prayer all their pains, their cares, the concerns of their families, their legitimate, profound, and apostolic ambitions.

Without the addition of the assembly's *silent* part, the celebrant ends up offering God only an empty—albeit majestic—formula.

### 3. Silence—for Reflection on the Word of God

At the conclusion of each reading and the homily, a word of the reader and the homilist will enable the people to meditate on the Word of God that has been communicated to them *here and now*, God's Word to them today. It is a Word that comes to them in the living event of the Church's Liturgy and makes Christ present to them.

In order that a real dialogue may ensue between them and Jesus now present, they must go out to meet Him in *sacred silence* of heart and mind; they must take hold of His Word and be completely open to it.

One celebrant allows a period of an Our Father to go by after each reading. This is only a suggestion. Each community can think up its own time referent and have the celebrant put it into use.

### 4. Silence—for Applying the Eucharist to Life

At the Prayer of the Faithful, a word from the celebrant can trigger a productive silence on the part of the people. Such a silence will enable them to once again exercise their general priesthood in praying for the Church, the world, and their own community and family.

The word may be something like: "Each of us may now add our own intentions in silence." Thus, every one present will be able to apply this particular Liturgy to his/her life. The Mass really touches the life of all present.

Then the concluding prayer means something to all present, establishing a closer bond between the celebrant and the assembly in the celebration.

### 5. Silence—for Offering Thanks and Praise with Christ

During the Eucharistic Prayer a brief admonition of the celebrant will enable the people to unite themselves with him as he pronounces the priestly prayer par excellence. He does so as the interpreter of the voice of God and the voice of the people who raise their hearts to God.

The celebrant can outline for the faithful the motives which the Eucharistic Prayer offers for thanksgiving, adapting them to his congregation, helping the people to realize that their own lives are involved in salvation history and thus to gain more fruit from the Eucharistic Prayer.

It is instructive to note that for nearly one thousand years the Eucharistic Prayer was recited *silently* by the celebrant, so that during this part of Mass there was total silence—broken only by the ringing of the bell at the Consecration. This custom of silent prayer appears to have arisen out of the desire to express and invoke an attitude of awe and loving fear toward the Eucharistic Mystery.

Yet originally the recitation had been carried out aloud in the name of the faithful. Therefore, in 1966 the recitation aloud was again prescribed by the Church—but the people were provided with *a time for liturgical silence*, a time for savoring the mystery, enhancing spiritual growth, and attaining closer union with God.

It is fairly easy for those in the assembly to recapture for themselves an attitude of holy awe as they listen to the recitation by the celebrant. They can then add to it their own loving submission to God as the fruit of their silence. This twofold attitude finds expression in the Memorial Acclamation which surges forth from their hearts and breaks that silence at the culminating point of the Eucharistic Prayer and in the Great Amen which erupts at the conclusion of the Canon.

### 6. Silence—for Dialoguing with Christ

After Communion, a remark of the celebrant may prod the people to make full use of the time to praise God in their hearts and to pray to the Eucharistic Lord whom they have just received in Communion—the bond of union for the community.

This period of silence will then get the people ready for the Prayer after Communion which expresses the people's prayer once again. It usually recalls the Gift they have just received and asks that this Gift may produce its fruits in them.

The people are urged to think of their daily lives and occupations and how to bring Christ there. "Union with Christ, to which the Sacrament itself is directed, is not to be limited to the duration of the celebration of the Eucharist; it is to be prolonged into the entire Christian life, in such a way that the Christian faithful, contemplating unceasingly the Gift they have received, may make their lives a continual thanksgiving under the guidance of the Holy Spirit and may produce fruits of greater charity."[34]

In some churches a custom has arisen of having a "Communion Meditation" for this purpose. This may or may not be the answer. But it does indicate the direction in which the Church wants such silence to go.

In recent years some Catholics have felt the loss of a sense of mystery at Mass as a result of the new rite. Regardless of the cause, it is obvious that we already have a remedy close at hand. We have at high points in the celebration built-in periods of liturgical silence. These represent golden opportunities for entering deeply into the mystery of God's salvation.

Thus, as the Eucharistic celebration is now structured there is a happy blend of times for spoken prayer and times for silent prayer. Unfortunately, many times these parts are not provided or not given their full length, and the people are deprived of an important value intended for them by the Church.

On the other side of the coin, even when silence is provided in the service, many among the people do not know what to do during what seems to be a lag in the public prayer. Hence, they do not take advantage of the means for spiritual growth put at their disposal by the Church.

Therefore, it is incumbent on every celebrant in conjunction with his Liturgy Committee to seek ways to make the most of silent times for his community. He must insure that the people will participate as fully as possible in the Eucharist—and not remain as mute spectators in the most important action of their lives.

In the words of the Foreword to the *American Sacramentary*: "The *proper use* of periods of silent prayer and reflection will help to render the celebration less mechanical and impersonal and lend a more prayerful spirit to the liturgical rite. Just as there should be no celebration without song, so too there should be no celebration without periods for silent prayer and reflection."

Chapter 9
# THE NEED FOR LITURGICAL CATECHESIS

A pastor in a large northeastern parish decided to adorn the *Lectionary for Mass* in the fashion of the ancient *Book of Gospels*. He overlaid it with a large ikon that was visible throughout the church. After Mass a few people inquired of members of the Liturgy Committee as to why the pastor had placed a picture of St. Augustine on the Book of Readings.

The members were not really sure until they checked with the chairperson. They then were told that it was not St. Augustine on the Book but Christ—who becomes present in the assembly when His Word is read. "But," the people retorted, "*it doesn't look like Christ!*" Thus, the catechetical action intended by the pastor had largely gone to waste—for the people were in the main unacquainted with the ikons of Jesus!

Such knowledge should be commonplace among practicing Christians. It is part of a general religious and liturgical culture that should flow from a lived Christian life. Why then is this lacking in most Christians today?

I dare say that the core of this little story could be multiplied many times over. Unfortunately, there are too many Catholics who are unaware of some of the fundamental symbols and truths of our faith. Those of us who are blessed with a good knowledge of the Faith take many things for granted. We should try to be cognizant of our Catholic culture and communicate it whenever we can.

### Salvation Revealed through Signs

Christianity has always been associated with a multiplicity of signs taken from the history of salvation. This is true of the Old Testament, the New Testament, and the time of the Church in which we now live.

Thus, all that takes place in the old dispensation is merely the sign of

God's salvation. It is discerned by faith alone which is capable of perceiving invisible realities in visible things.

The entire history of Israel and the whole of the inspired scriptures constitute a sign of God's salvation, since we see or discern one reality in them while our faith must grasp quite another reality. We see a people among other peoples, with its own culture, customs, and national history; we see men among other men, with their own language and personal history; we record political, social, and individual facts. These all appear at first glance to be very human realities. But through the ministry of the prophetic word, Israel is alerted that they are not purely natural events at all: "Hear, O Israel, . . . I am the Lord your God, who brought you out of the land of Egypt" (Dt 5:6). Victories and defeats of Israel or prophetic oracles are by no means merely the deeds or the discourses of man but the acts and words of God.[35]

In the New Testament, we see one thing in the Gospel but another thing that must be grasped by faith.

In the flesh of an infant, God causes his own glory to dwell; in a Son of Man, the Father sends us his own Son. In the actions of the incarnate Word, in his miracles and person, the Messianic work is manifested, and his words are Good News of Salvation.[36]

In the time of the Church after Jesus' Ascension and the Coming of the Holy Spirit, this same language of signs continues to hold true. What was visible in the person of Jesus has now passed into the mysteries, that is, into the sacred signs and sacraments of the Church.

The visible Church . . . is the sign of the risen Lord . . . by her nature as a society of believers, since the latter are invisible members of the Mystical Body whose Head is Christ. Again, she is a sign of Christ by reason of the twofold trust through which she communicates the grace of salvation. The first is Sacred Scripture. Under the sign of a human word, the Holy Spirit whom Jesus has sent us from the Father enables us to hear the word of God. The Sacraments of the Divine Life constitute the second. Under the sign of water we receive the Divine adoption and under the sign of bread we are nourished with eternal life.[37]

This still does not exhaust the area in which sacred signs impart Christian knowledge and grace. Besides the sacraments, for the person who lives through the Church in the risen Lord, everything in the world becomes by means of faith the sign of the new life inaugurated in the Paschal Mystery.

## The Divine in Human Experience

There exists a kind of first order of sacred sign in creation. This refers to what the Fathers of the Church termed the "vestiges" and images of God. For example, there is a vestige of God in the light—a sign of His glorious splendor and ardent love; in the stability of the firmament and the earth—signs of His truth and fidelity; in the waters—which give life; and in the wind—which none can see. Finally, there is an image of God in human beings made after the likeness of God—in their power to know good and evil and in the love that binds them to their fellow humans.

Furthermore, Jesus Himself made use of natural signs to impart His message of salvation as well as that salvation itself. He used water, a sign of death and life, to make us die to the life of sin and be born to the life of the Spirit. He used a meal, a sign of fraternal communion, to institute the sacrament of unity in His love. The language of faith is thus completely made up of natural signs of God and religious mysteries in the world.

What this really amounts to is the fact that there are in human experiences a great variety of vestiges of God if only they are perceived. Almost everything in a person's life can be made to reflect the Divinity in some way or other. That is one of the reasons why there has been such a tremendous accentuation of human experience in present-day religious writing.

This factor was picked up by the Second Vatican Council and made almost a "locus" (or source) of theology.[38] Everything in the world can be used to impart the message of Revelation provided it is used in the right manner. In the words of Father Gelineau:

> All the events of our Christian life—in the measure in which they are read in the light of faith in the dead and risen Christ; all our visible activities whether spiritual or temporal—in the measure in which they are filled with love for Christ offering Himself to His Father—also constitute for us in their way expressive signs of the language of the God Who saves and sanctifies the world.[39]

## The Liturgical Language of Symbolism

As a result of the factors mentioned above, the Liturgy of the Church is itself replete with a language of symbolism. Some of it comes from the Biblical symbolism and some from the ordinary life of the people of the times in which the liturgical rites were put together. Thus, this liturgical language is an elaborated language—much more historical than natural, much more personal than physical and much more social than individual.

Through this liturgical language and its rite, God is worshiped, and human beings receive sanctification as well as enlightenment concerning the true relation between God and themselves. And this is all effected through Jesus Christ, the Christian Symbol par excellence and God's definitive Word to humankind.

> Jesus Christ is God's unsurpassable, definitive Word to mankind, which, though prepared and uttered in a particular historical setting, so far transcends it—given God's universal salvific will and the consecration of all that is human by Christ's Incarnation and Resurrection—that the historical forms of the Jewish-Hellenistic world have no abiding validity.[40]

The sacraments, for example, contain two aspects: (1) the reality accomplished which is in continuity with the works of God in the two Testaments, and (2) the visible sign—water, bread, oil, baptizing, feasting, anointing—by means of which the action of God operates. Both of these aspects are symbolized by action and/or word.

Thus, in any liturgical celebration there is a great amount of latent communication that is presented to the worshipers and this entails a dedicated attempt at a hermeneutics of the liturgical rite. Such a hermeneutics involves many factors and meanings and must view the totality of the rite, not only the words and gestures.

In our time, there is a huge emphasis on updating the liturgical rites so that they will be intelligible to the modern person. The reasons for their unintelligibility are many, mainly due to the lack of a religious culture, as already mentioned. The modern person has lost the sense of the Bible as well as the sense of the language of the Liturgy, which is basically made up of the terms used in non-urban societies.

### The Liturgy as the Fount of Catechesis

Liturgy may be termed the culminating expression of tradition and life. As such, it is an inexhaustible source of catechesis in the Church. It enables us to gather together into one all the aspects of the Mystery of

Christ, by speaking in concrete terms to the mind as well as to the senses.

The Liturgy is made up of readings, chants, and prayers—but it is much more than these. It is an *action*—an action of life. Even when we simply refer to the Liturgy, we regard it as the sum of religious elements in which we take a lively part and of activities which we ourselves posit. The Liturgy demands a participation that is the most conscious, active, communitarian, full and fruitful. For God wants us to be His collaborators in the work that He accomplishes for our salvation.

The Liturgy is *catechesis in action*. It celebrates and expresses the Mystery of Christ as a mystery of salvation that is realized today in the Church, in a sacramental, significative, and efficacious action. A lively participation in the Liturgical Action enables believers to penetrate even more deeply into the Mystery of Christ, and to comprehend its extension and its wondrous unity.

The new Eucharistic Prayers nicely underscore the convergence of creational revelation and biblical revelation in the Paschal Mystery as well as the unity of the salvific initiative that the Father pursues through the work of the Son and in the Holy Spirit with loving determination until the end of time. All of this is highly instructive and formative since it is expressed in a prayer of praise.

Moreover, the whole past and future of the History of Salvation are concentrated in the *present* of the Liturgical Celebrations, of the Eucharist and all the sacraments. At the same time, the worshiping community and the individual members gather the fruits of the Redemption, and commit themselves to insure that it is extended ever more to humanity for eternal life. This attitude is expressed in a universal form especially in the Eucharistic Prayer. In the Prayer of the Faithful it is set forth in a more local form, in keeping with the needs of the moment and those of the concrete praying community.

Thus, the Liturgy is rendered actual and made a vital part of the lives of those who participate in it. When properly understood, this aspect constitutes the greatest catechesis of all.

The ultimate reason why the Liturgy is a fount of catechesis is that it is a *living catechesis*, a *teaching in action*. This makes it a marvelous instrument for Christian formation—one which cannot be attained in any other Christian discipline. Pope Pius XI made this point when he called the Liturgy the forum where "the ordinary and privileged teaching of the Church is given":

> For people are instructed in the truths of faith and brought to ap-

preciate the inner joys of religion far more effectually by the annual celebration of our sacred Mysteries than by any pronouncement, however weighty, of the teaching of the Church.

Such pronouncements usually reach only a few and the more learned among the faithful. Feasts reach all the faithful. Pronouncements speak but once. Feasts speak every year—in fact, forever. The Church's teaching affects the mind primarily. Her feasts affect both mind and heart, and have a salutary effect upon the whole of a person's nature.

People are composed of body and soul. Thus, they need the external festivities [of the Liturgy], so that the sacred rites—in all their beauty and variety—may stimulate them to drink more deeply of the fountain of God's teaching, that they may make it a part of themselves, and use it with profit for their spiritual lives.[41]

Over the course of the centuries, the Church has made good use of the Liturgy in just this way—guided always by the Spirit who has been given to her. Thus, in the earliest days of the Christian era, when Christians were suffering cruel persecution, the cult of the Martyrs was begun in the Liturgy so that—in the words of St. Augustine—"the feasts of the Martyrs might inspire the people to martyrdom." Later, the liturgical honors paid to confessors, virgins, and holy women produced wonderful fruit in an increased zest for virtue.

Finally, the feasts instituted in honor of Mary led the people to have greater devotion to her as their ever-present advocate and love her more deeply as a Mother bequeathed to them by their Redeemer.

## Catechetics of the Liturgy

If the Liturgy is to be a fount of catechesis there must first be a *catechesis of the Liturgy*. Unfortunately, one of the negative side effects of the magnificent liturgical renewal initiated by the Second Vatican Council has been the decline of liturgical catechesis. This consequence was in no way intended by the Council, as is evidenced by its explicit declaration of the catechetical riches found in the Liturgy:

> Although the sacred Liturgy is above all the worship of the Divine Majesty, *it likewise contains abundant instruction* for the faithful. . . . Not only when things are read "which have been written for our instruction" (Rm 15:4), but also when the Church prays and sings or

## The Need for Liturgical Catechesis 77

acts, the faith of those taking part is nourished and their souls are raised to God.[42]

Accordingly the Council called for rites that are intelligible to the people so that this catechesis can take place more easily. Indeed the rites have been remodeled, made more understandable, rendered less complex.

However, the instant catechesis so confidently expected by all who were involved in the early reform of the Liturgy has not materialized. If anything, the people seem more devoid than ever of liturgical and Christian knowledge.

One of the major reasons for this lack is the implementation of the Conciliar teaching itself. The rites are so simple that it is easy to assume the people will automatically understand them, *without the need for extensive catechesis*.

As a result, most Catholic schools place little emphasis on teaching the Liturgy through the use of Missals (or Missalettes). Children receive scant instruction about liturgical culture. They grow up thinking they know the Mass—but they are sorely deficient in that knowledge.

### Guidelines for Liturgical Catechesis

Genuine liturgical catechesis cannot fail to yield rich rewards. We should stress that the Liturgy is a *dialogue in action*. God is intervening through the Liturgy in our lives today. We too, then, are part of Salvation History.

The Liturgy sweeps us up into this History. Liturgical Celebrations constitute a *profession of faith* in action. The liturgical texts themselves are richly interwoven with Biblical expressions and become precious formulas for faith and prayer.

The liturgical prayers and chants inculcate spiritual attitudes of filial piety, adoration, thanksgiving, offering, and contrition. They express in praise and prayer the most vivid sentiments of faith, hope, and love of believers.

The Sacred Congregation for Divine Worship has counseled[43] all to be mindful that the liturgical renewal should be a concern of the whole Church. At pastoral meetings, therefore, this renewal should be *studied in both its theoretical and its practical aspects as an instrument for the Christian formation of the people*, so that the Liturgy may become for them a living and meaningful experience.

Pastors should consider themselves above all as ministers of the community's Liturgy. They should be exemplars for the people by their *generous fidelity* to the norms and directions of the Church, and by their *spirit of faith*.

They should constantly deepen their own understanding of the liturgical mysteries, and should strive to communicate this understanding to the faithful. They will thus contribute to that growth and progress of the Church which is the fruit of the renewed Liturgy—a Liturgy which is open to the needs of our times and yet far removed from every kind of secularism and individualism.

Pastors have a golden opportunity for liturgical catechesis *within the Liturgy itself*. They can make use of *admonitions* at important parts of the liturgical action. They can give a brief introduction to the celebration inserting it into the Liturgical Year of the Church—indicating what attitude the particular service is trying to inculcate in the people.

They can also situate the readings for the people. A judicious word will provide a minimum Biblical knowledge that will enable the listeners to respond more deeply and positively to God's Word (and His presence among them in that Word) on the day in question.

The Homily provides a special time for instruction and enlightenment. Pastors can clarify liturgical signs and actions, inculcating in their people liturgical attitudes and enabling them to apply the Liturgy to their lives.

Again, before the Eucharistic Prayer, celebrants can bring the people into the action by pointing out the particular reason for offering thanks and praise to God through Christ on that day—for celebrating the living Memorial of Christ's Death and Resurrection.

*Apart from the celebration*, the greatest way to impart liturgical catechesis is by seeing that the liturgies are well prepared. This means getting together a Liturgy Committee that is a true cross-section of the community and working with its members to devise celebrations that will be particularly geared for the parish.

We are not speaking here at all about doing anything against liturgical rules, such as "underground" liturgies. These are in the long run self-defeating besides being a disservice to the people—substituting chaff for the wheat of true Liturgy.

What we are talking about is tailoring the Eucharistic Celebrations to one's community by taking full advantage of the options that are built into the Liturgy—*precisely for this purpose*. This means everything from choosing the right hymns for the community to composing truly relevant petitions for the Prayer of the Faithful—petitions that will be appreciated by the community in question for they affect that community.

Other ways of communicating liturgical catechesis are through the school, through arranging little "Liturgy Meetings" for the parishioners from time to time, and through running articles on Liturgy in the Parish Bulletin or Monthly Newsletter.

### Goal of Liturgical Catechesis

No matter what approach is taken, the goal of any kind of liturgical catechesis should never be lost sight of. The ultimate purpose of any liturgical celebration is that it be lived—that it not be left behind in church when the people return home.

A liturgical catechesis which would fail to help bring Christ into their everyday lives would be a false catechesis. The truths that are made known to our minds must move our hearts and our wills and bring them into line with God's saving plan. In short, they must inculcate in us a kind of liturgical spirituality.

Every catechesis should lead us to greater participation in the Liturgy. In turn, every Liturgy should enable us to bring our Christian witness to the world—through our "liturgized" lives. This "living the Liturgy" will then reach full cycle with our more active participation in our next Liturgy.

In this way those who practice this liturgical spirituality will bear greater fruits for the Church and for themselves. They will enable the Church to permeate the life and habits of all peoples as well as their own private and family lives and the social, economic, and political life of their immediate surroundings.

In the words of Pope John Paul II, "devotion to the Eucharist is not so much a cult of the inaccessibly transcendent as it is a worship of God's kindness and goodness, and, at the same time, a merciful and redemptive transformation of the world in the heart of the human person."[44]

Not only does the Eucharist perfect that image of God which we bear within us and which corresponds to the image Christ has revealed to us. It also educates us regarding love for our neighbor, showing us how important every human being is in God's sight—since Christ offers Himself to each equally under the appearances of bread and wine. Ultimately the understanding of the Eucharistic Mystery impels us to love our neighbor and indeed to love every human person.

Chapter 10
# LITURGICAL ADAPTATION: CELEBRATIONS OF MAJOR AMERICAN HOLIDAYS

The Church has always been most careful to apply liturgical celebrations to the life of her people. Each age presents new circumstances, novel approaches, and different ways of life for human beings. The Church gears her Liturgy to Christianize those circumstances, approaches and ways that touch the heart of her people.

In the early days, she Christianized pagan feasts, instituting the Feast of Christmas in place of the festival of the Winter Solstice in honor of the pagan gods and setting up Ember Days in place of the pagan agricultural festivals (sowing time, the corn harvest and vintage time).

In the Middle Ages, the Church encouraged the rise of the guilds as an aid to the ordinary person. At the same time, she began to include in her Liturgy the feasts of various patrons of those guilds who were solemnly honored by the guild members.

In our day, the Church is seeking to Christianize the major holidays of the civil year, such as Washington's Birthday, Memorial Day, and especially Independence Day, Labor Day and Thanksgiving Day. Such days are becoming very important holidays for all Americans, and the Church wants to insure that Catholics will take full advantage of their faith at such times by inserting them directly in Salvation History.

The new *Sacramentary* contains special Mass texts for Independence Day, Labor Day and Thanksgiving Day. In this way we can combine our religious faith with our patriotic fervor and give glory to God while honoring our country. We can be living the Liturgy to the full.

Hence, a careful consideration of these three new liturgical celebrations is sure to yield much food for thought and tell us a great deal about the particular impact of the themes of these great holidays on our lives. From among many approaches, we can choose the following—each tailored to the particular tack taken by the Church in developing the new texts.

### Independence Day Liturgy

Independence Day (July 4) is kept in memory of the gallant struggle of our forebears to attain freedom from an oppressive tyranny, freedom to have certain inalienable rights which our Creator conferred on all human beings—among which are life, liberty, and the pursuit of happiness.

It is interesting to note that these three rights are precisely the ones that Jesus upheld for all when He went about proclaiming the Good News. "I have come that they may have *life* and have it more abundantly" (Jn 10:10). "The truth shall set you *free*" (Mt 8:32). "If the Son frees you, you will really be *free*" (Jn 8:36). And our Lord's magnificent Sermon on the Mount outlines the program that leads to true *happiness*: "*Happy* are the poor in spirit . . . " (Mt 5:2-12).

Thus, there is a natural affinity between our Independence Day and our spiritual independence. There is also a natural affinity between our celebration of independence and the Jewish memorial of their freedom from Egyptian bondage which initiated their national beginnings. God guided that chosen band of people into the promised land and He surely guided our forebears into making the United States "one nation under God with liberty and justice for all."

Admittedly, there are injustices that are created—and they are most regrettable. But the fact remains that the United States is almost alone in the world in its veritable passion for justice for all regardless of race, creed, or color. This was vividly brought home to me once again in a recent assignment of jury duty bringing me face to face with the unstinting desire for strict justice that pervaded the courts—in spite of cost, personal inconveniences, or official embarrassments of any kind.

It is well for us to remember such things on this national holiday and the Liturgy can be of inestimable help in doing so. The Church has wisely provided a Mass for Independence Day that takes cognizance of the American Dream and exalts the thirst for social justice found therein.

In the official Prayer for the day the Church asks us to open our hearts to greater love for his Son and to ensure that the boundaries of nations will not set limits to our love. Instead, may they give us courage to build a land that serves Him in *truth and justice*.

## Liturgical Adaptation: Celebrations of Major American Holidays

Then in the beautiful Preface, composed especially for this Mass under the guidance of the American Bishops and approved by the Holy Father, the Church alludes more specifically to our nation's origin and purpose. We thank God and give Him praise for His Son who spoke to human beings a message of *peace* and taught us to live as brothers and sisters. *His message took form in the vision of our fathers as they fashioned a nation whose people might live as one.* This message lives on in our midst as a task for people today and a promise for tomorrow.

We have a beautiful base on which to build powerful and meaningful liturgies on this national holiday. We should utilize the prescribed texts, making a judicious selection from among the various options provided by the Liturgy, and enlist the creativity of our Liturgical Committees (in accord with liturgical rules) to make our July 4 Eucharistic Celebration come alive for our people.

In this respect, I have a graphic recollection of what one Liturgy Committee did to help associate July 4 with the Liturgy for its community. The festive liturgy was concelebrated by all the priests of the parish and fully participated in by the people with songs and responses, inner silence and outward actions. The readers were well prepared and the ceremony was clearly inspiring, culminating with Communion under both kinds.

On entering the church, each person had been given a small piece of paper and told to pocket it until further advised in the service. Now, during the after-Communion meditation the first reader addressed the people briefly. He pointed out the connection of the holiday with the Liturgy and then noted that every paper handed out had one of the first ten Amendments to the Constitution typed on it.

He was now going to read each one and as he did so each person who had the particular Amendment should stand while it was read—and then remain standing until all were read. It seems so simple. Yet for those who were there it became a towering experience in which Liturgy and life were inextricably entwined. Never had I realized, for example, the religious aspect of the American Dream. Never had I fully appreciated how much in tune with the human spirit was our faith.

All who attended have remained steadfast in the opinion that such a Liturgy was unique and most relevant. When Liturgy is carried out in this way, it gives the lie to all those excuses that are put forth about the new Liturgy—that it is boring, has lost the sense of mystery, and in general misses the boat. Such a Liturgy shows that the very opposite is true.

We have a very magnetic Liturgy—if only it is carried out as intended by the Church. The July 4th Eucharist can be made vital—but so can every Eucharist—by the dedication and creativity of Catholics which are called for by the liturgical rules. Americans are noted for their resourcefulness. It would be wonderful if every July 4 all of us would try to make the Eucharist live for us and relate it to our lives in this Land of Promise.

### Labor Day Liturgy

The Liturgy for Labor Day provides an object lesson in the concern that the Church has for us. At times the Liturgy is derided and the charge is leveled that it does not correspond with the needs of the people. The Labor Day Liturgy gives the lie to such charges. Especially composed for the United States, the liturgical texts provide a "concise theology of labor." The following remarks give only a brief indication of the wealth of spiritual ideas found in the Mass for Labor Day.

1) *God is the ultimate source of all creativity.* "May the goodness of the Lord . . . give success to the work of our hands" (Entrance Antiphon). "Lord, give success to the work of our hands" (Responsorial Psalm).

2) *We are God's co-workers although we can do nothing by ourselves.* "By the labor of man you govern and guide to perfection the work of creation" (Opening Prayer—A). "You have placed all the powers of nature under the control of man and his work" (Opening Prayer—B).

3) *Work enhances human beings.* "Give all men work that enhances their human dignity" (Opening Prayer—A, alternate).

4) *Human labor joins us to Christ's saving action.* "Lord, . . . by the human labor we offer you join us to the saving work of Christ" (Prayer over the Gifts—B).

5) *Work builds up God's Kingdom.* "Lord, by doing the work you have entrusted to us, may we sustain our life on earth and build up your kingdom in faith" (Prayer after Communion—A).

6) *Labor in common leads to unity and brotherly love.* "May we . . . work with our brothers and sisters at our common task, establishing true love" (Opening Prayer—B).

7) *The earth has been given into human hands to cultivate.* "The Lord God then took the man and settled him in the garden of Eden to cultivate and care for it" (Reading I—Gn 2:4-9, 15).

8) *Work is a necessity for life.* "Anyone who will not work should not eat" (Reading II—2 Th 3:6-12, 16).

## Liturgical Adaptation: Celebrations of Major American Holidays 85

9) *Work is never an end in itself but is always related to God's plan for us; it should be carried out with detachment and dependence on God.* "Seek first [God's] kingdom over you, his way of holiness, and all these things will be given you besides" (Gospel—Mt 6:31-34).

However, the Church is a wise mother and she has left room in the Liturgy for the modern idea that labor is more than just work. It can also apply to any activity. We labor at planting a garden, we labor at bowling, mountain climbing, and at a hundred other types of activity. We would call any one of these a "labor of love."

In other words, labor can also refer to leisure activities. That is what Jesus tries to tell us in the Gospel for Labor Day. Do not let labor consume you. Rather be a little lighthearted about it. Leave room for meditation (for God) and for play (for yourself).

In this respect, Father Thomas Kilduff has provided us with some excellent insights on labor and leisure:

> Leisure is every bit as important as work and not unrelated to it as human activity. The key to meaningful leisure is the ability to play. Our vocabulary reflects the healthy influence of work and play, the mutual interaction of the two and their reciprocal enrichment. We speak of a mechanic "tinkering" with machines, a research engineer "playing around" with various experiments, a financier "playing the market," and a philosopher "playing with ideas."
>
> Truly human work, though it cost man something, is like play, free in the sense that it truly comes from within as a realization of the human potential. Such work is an expression of freedom and joy, which is just what play is.[45]

All of these ideas can be found in the Liturgy chosen by the Church for Labor Day. They are themes that provide food for thought over a wide period of time.

In this way, the Church helps us to keep our perspective about labor, about the world, about salvation, about leisure, and about our ultimate goal.

In the light of such facts, it becomes all too clear that it is not the Liturgy that has nothing to say to us but we who do not know how to take advantage of what it has to say. If we learn to listen to it with faith by taking our full part in each celebration, we will not only receive much grace but a good deal of valuable catechesis as well.

## Thanksgiving Day Liturgy

Contrary to what some would aver, the Church must constantly speak to the people of her day. She must *adapt* herself to every age—without losing any part of the substance of her message. For adaptation is a rule of life for any living creature.

The only question is what determines true adaptation and what is false adaptation. The Church has set down rules for adaptation and in recent years has shown adaptation in action via the Liturgy. In the present instance, the Church has taken an American civil-religious festival and fashioned a Liturgy for it that respects both the civil character and the religious aspect.

Governor William Bradford of Plymouth Colony instituted the original festival in 1621. Ever since then United States citizens have cherished Thanksgiving Day. This custom spread throughout the British North American colonies. During the Revolutionary War the Continental Congress adopted it, and the states observed the day thereafter.

President Abraham Lincoln designated this day as a national holiday. In 1941, a joint resolution of Congress fixed the fourth Thursday of November as the national day of thanksgiving.

Now the Thanksgiving Day Liturgy inserted in the new *Sacramentary* by the Church has become one of the best examples of liturgical creativity. Naturally, the essentials of the Eucharist remain the same as for other days. The texts chosen obey the rules of the *Roman Missal*—the Readings are from Sacred Scripture, the Antiphons are adapted from Biblical texts, and the presidential Prayers are permeated with Biblical allusions.

In addition, the new creations (presidential Prayers, the Prayer of the Faithful, and the Preface) are splendid examples of adapting the themes of the American festival to the Liturgy. In this respect, they render innocuous the complaint that the Church is not adapting to the cultures of her people.

The Opening Prayer recalls the notion of America populated by a covenanted society. It stresses gratitude to God for all His gifts (including the gift to be part of a society dedicated to service of one another). At the same time, it asks for the grace of openness to concern for others and sharing God's gift with one another.

The Prayer of the Faithful in brief but pithy language provides our proper response for the material and spiritual gifts given our country and the opportunity of rendering God thanks for them. It calls for recognizing the needs of other people and responding to them, that the wealth and resources of our nation may be a blessing for all of us, and that the Eucharist may always be the source and expression of our thanksgiving. Its concluding prayer succinctly expresses the theme for Thanksgiving Day—that we may love creation as God loves it and so prepare for the feast of everlasting thanksgiving.

The newly composed Preface puts the finishing touches to the masterful rite that has been formulated. It thus gives the particular reason for our present Eucharist and inserts the American experience into the History of Salvation in a concrete and understandable fashion. This splendid example of a Preface recalls the history of salvation that would make all human beings blessed and free in Jesus. Then it indicates that this very thing happened to the fathers of our American democracy, for they "came to this land as if out of the desert into a place of promise and hope." In other words, their dream too was inspired by God and was directed to God.

This same salvation experience did not end with our fathers. "It happens to us still, in our time, as you lead all (human beings) through Your Church to the blessed vision of peace." Through our lives, through our country, we too are inserted into Salvation History and are on our way to final union with God. It is for this that we give thanks through the present Eucharist.

The *readings* are judiciously chosen. All communicate the theme of thanksgiving for blessings received. At the same time, each accentuates one of the many qualities of true thanksgiving. As such, these readings may be termed a little treatise on thanksgiving that will impart greater understanding of this theme to those who carefully read the texts in private and listen wholeheartedly to them during the celebration.

There are six passages from the Old Testament, four from St. Paul, and three from the Gospels.

*Isaiah* (63:7-9) delineates God's *love in act* toward those of His children who remain *loyal* to Him. Theme: thanksgiving entails loyalty to God for His gifts.

*Solomon* (1 K 8:55-61) speaking at the height of Israel's material prosperity praises God for His goodness to Israel in terms of material and spiritual things, and calls for *fidelity* to God. Theme: thanksgiving entails fidelity to the God who has given us wondrous gifts.

*Sirach* (50:22-24) conjures up God's creative might and providence in looking after the human beings He has made, and calls upon all of them—His joy, peace, and enduring goodness. Theme: thanksgiving entails praise for God's might and providence.

*Joel* (2:21-24, 26-29) reminds the people of God's goodness in sending "the teacher of justice" and material prosperity and most of all in granting them His *presence*. Theme: thanksgiving entails exaltation for God's presence.

*Zephaniah* (3:14-15) calls upon the people to thank God for taking away their sins, *saving them from their enemies*, and being in their very midst. Theme: thanksgiving entails elimination of fear.

*Paul* (1 Cor 1:3-9) praises God for giving us a Christian culture ("every gift of speech and knowledge") and setting us on a *solid Christian course* toward the Second Coming. Theme: thanksgiving is best shown by a life dedicated to God.

In *Ephesians* (1:3-14) Paul goes on to stress that God has given us every *spiritual blessing in Christ*—indeed Christianity in our country is flourishing. Theme: thanksgiving is always made *in Christ*.

In *Colossians* (3:12-17) Paul tells us we must put on Christian virtues *founded on love* and do everything in the Name of the Lord. Theme: thanksgiving must ultimately be based on love.

In *First Timothy* (6:6-11, 17-19) Paul warns of the evil effects that stem from *material prosperity*. Theme: thanksgiving is genuine when it is combined with good works.

The *Responsorial Psalms* are all appropriate thanksgiving hymns and highlight one or other of the thanksgiving themes presented (for God's kindness and truth—1 Ch 29; for His Providence—Ps 113; for His wondrous deeds—Ps 145).

The *Alleluia Verses* remind us that true thanksgiving gives rise to praise for God because of His spiritual blessings in Christ (Ep 1:3), leads to rich harvests (Ps 126:5), calls for continuous praise (1 Th 5:18), and voices the Church's worship of God (Ambrosian hymn).

The *Gospel Readings* form the culmination of this thanksgiving teaching. *Luke* (12:15-21) tells us of the foolish rich man who lives only for his riches with no thought of using his goods for others. The sudden death that deprives him of his "security" shows that we should be *secure in the Lord* while using our riches unselfishly. Theme: thanksgiving entails sharing goods.

*Mark* (5:18-20) tells the story of the cured demoniac who wanted to accompany Jesus. Our Lord does not dissuade him from being His follower—but points him in another direction. He tells the man to bring the Good News to the deprived people of his pagan region. Theme: thanksgiving entails sharing one's faith.

*Luke* (17:11-19) tells the story of ten lepers who are cured but only one comes back to give thanks to Jesus. He demonstrates the importance of showing gratitude in our lives. Theme: thanksgiving must be translated into action.

### Varied Liturgical Analyses

The three analyses made above are based on three different approaches to liturgical feasts and texts. The first analyzes overall themes of an adapted liturgical celebration. It shows how such celebrations have the power to apply Liturgy to the everyday life of the people. In this way, the Liturgy, will become the driving force it should be in the lives of all who celebrate it fully, actively, and consciously.

The second analyzes one main thought of an adapted liturgical celebration. It shows the wealth of Christian teaching that is found in the liturgical texts on a subject of great concern to people of our day. Such an analysis clearly demonstrates the power that such a Liturgy can wield in making the faith of the people come alive not only in the hearts and minds of the people but in their actions as well.

The third analysis gives a brief commentary of the liturgical texts. In doing so, it sheds light on the different nuances of the important subject with which the particular Liturgy deals. It provides ample evidence that the Liturgical texts when properly chosen and adapted to the feasts of a people can both enlighten and inspire.

No matter which method is followed, a careful consideration of the Church's Liturgy always yields many benefits. For the plain truth is that in the Liturgy we encounter Christ who is still preaching His Gospel to us and applying His Redemption to the whole of our lives.

Chapter 11

# CHRIST IN THE LITURGY: THE EXPECTATION OF THE NATIONS

You may have heard bandied the slogan: "Jesus, yes—the Church, no!" For reasons too varied and too numerous to deal with here, people feel justified in bypassing the Church to get to Christ. They run after all who claim to bring Christ to them without a Church.

Sadly, by rejecting the Church these people are also turning their backs on the best means of getting in touch with Christ, the very person they are seeking. The Church is the community of faith that stretches back to Christ's First Coming and looks forward to His Second Coming. In the meantime it has the power to bring us to Christ in the present.

Through the Liturgy the Church enables us to encounter Christ today. When we reflect on this thought, we are almost overwhelmed by it. We can be in touch with the one who was the *Expectation of the Nations*. What a wondrous gift.

We do not reach Him in the manner of those who were alive during His earthly life. In a way, we reach Him in the manner that those who came before Him reached Him—*in desire*. Our desire is more informed and more specific but it must also be more devout.

Those who went before Christ reached out to Him vaguely with the limited information that they had about Him. They looked to Him in spite of trials and tribulations, rumors and misconceptions of all kinds. In some wonderful way they attained some part of the Coming Redeemer.

The Church has always regarded Jesus Christ as the Messiah foretold by the Prophets of the Old Testament. At the same time, she has also pointed Him out as the *Expectation of the Nations*—the One who was eagerly though implicitly awaited by all nations.

As the joyous feast of our Lord's Nativity comes around once again, we may draw benefit from considering this aspect of His coming. Such a consideration can give us a better appreciation of what Jesus has meant to the world.

### The World at the Time of Christ's Coming

When Jesus was born a profound peace filled the earth—the "pax Romana" (the peace of Rome). Rome ruled the world and maintained peace from the Rhone River in what is now France to the Indus River in India. Within subjugated nations there were, of course, pockets of resistance. Some planned and carried out guerrilla warfare. Overall, there was quiet.

Rome was also the guarantor of public order and unity. It constructed fast sea lanes and a wide network of roads linking inner lands with sea ports, so that transportation and commerce flourished. It made possible a kind of middle-class, made up of "free people" by birth or enfranchisement, and these enjoyed more benefits than ever before.

There was also prevalent a cultural unity brought about by the conquests of Alexander the Great two hundred years previously and the dynasties that succeeded him.

There was a religious feeling in the air that God listens to the poor, dispenses justice and mercy, and holds out the hope of deliverance. Most of the Roman subject nations preserved the hope of a divine messenger or intervention that would set them free and bring happiness to them. They harbored a religious "expectation."

The *Babylonians* were awaiting a time of happiness that would arrive after a time of evil. They expected a kind of Messianic Age, and in some quarters they even looked for some type of Savior.

The *Egyptians* nourished an expectation that can be traced back in some fashion to 1300 B.C. They awaited a king, beloved by all, who would conquer invaders and restore the sanctuaries that had been carted away to foreign countries. A new age of happiness was coming when even the natural order of things would be reestablished.

The *Persians* expected a powerful hero and sage similar to Zoroaster. By his blessed look on all creatures, he would unite them and raise the dead. At the same time, he would establish the kingdom of God.

The *ancient Romans* also expected a similar savior. As the historian Tacitus states: "People were generally convinced that the East was to prevail and Judea was to give rise to the Master and Ruler of the world."

## Christ in the Liturgy: The Expectation of the Nations

This tradition is also found in Suetonius, another Roman author: "There was an ancient and continuing belief throughout the East that the Jews were to attain the highest power—and this was based on prophecies that were certain."

The *Chinese* also believed that a great Wise Man would come—but in their case he would be from the West! Their sacred books tell of a bright light that would inaugurate the coming of the great Saint of the West whose religion was to be introduced into their country.

The *Hindus* believed that the supreme God Vishnu would reveal himself to human beings in ten successive incarnations. In the eighth he manifested himself in the person of the divine hero Krishna. The ninth incarnation took place in *Buddha*. The tenth was to take place in the future and be the most important one of all. Vishnu would appear in person and defend the good and destroy evil. He would bring about a new world and establish an era of happiness.

The *ancient Germanic tribes* had a mythology that looked forward to the end of the present world and its renewal with an era of happiness to follow.

The *Greeks* expected a great Saint of the West, for Aeschylus wrote: "Look not for any end, moreover, to this curse until God appears, to accept in his hand the pangs of your own sins vicariously."

### Virgil—the "Gentile Prophet" of Jesus

The *Romans of Christ's day* expected a King whom they had to recognize "to be sacred," in the words of Cicero. But their expectation had an even stronger base in the writings of the great poet Virgil, who died within the last two decades before Christ.

Between 42 and 37 B.C. Virgil composed ten Eclogues or Bucolics, pastoral poems in dactylic hexameters. In the *Fourth Eclogue* he described the birth of a divinely descended child who would bring peace to the world and usher in a kind of golden age.

Virgil spoke of a king in conjunction with a Virgin smiling favorably on her infant son "under whom the iron age will come to an end." The child's cradle would be a cornucopia of flowers and his coming would free the flocks from fear.

Gentile readers of the *Fourth Eclogue* would quickly regard the Child placed in a manger and honored by shepherds as a parallel to the dreamed-of child heralded by Virgil. It is little wonder then that in antiquity Virgil was classed among the Prophets by some Fathers of the Church, for he vividly recalls Isaiah's prophecy about the wonder-Child, Emmanuel.

The outstanding example of this worldwide expectation on the part of the nations is provided by the Magi who came seeking the "King of the Jews" after Christ's birth. They were astrologers from the East, and there is a story that a horoscope of the expected Messiah-King was circulating at the time of our Lord's coming.

The Magi are traditionally cited as three but they have been numbered as high as twelve in the history of the Church. They were most likely members of an ancient priestly class from Mesopotamia with a reputation as men who had access to supernatural knowledge.

Their idea of the Messiah-King could have been based on the Jewish expectation. After the Bible was translated into Greek (known as the *Septuagint*) two centuries before Christ, the Jewish expectation spread throughout the Greek-speaking world, and became known to educated people.

No matter where this expectation of the Magi originated, however, it was present at the time of Christ's birth. The actions of the Magi in journeying so far and so determinedly bear eloquent witness to the motivating force of such an expectation.

### Christ—the Center of Time

All the above should be a vivid reminder of God's plan for the world in Christ, of the uniqueness of Christ, and of the need of Christ for all people. God created all in view of Christ. Everything that went before Him looked toward Him and everything that has come after Him looks back to Him.

The endless ages that preceded the birth of Christ are not devoid of Him—they are impregnated with His influence. It was the ferment of His conception that set the cosmic masses moving and controlled the first currents of the biosphere. It was the preparation of His birth that accelerated the progress of instinct and the full development of thought on earth.

His coming called for all the fearsome, anonymous toil of primitive humanity, for the long drawn-out beauty of Egypt, for Israel's anxious expectation, for the slowly distilled fragrance of Eastern mysticism, and for the endlessly refined wisdom of the Greeks and the Romans.

We have much in common with the peoples of the nations who looked toward Christ in ancient times. But we are also more fortunate. Our faith is based on many more tangibles. It is enlightened, strong, and well-founded. When coupled with the Liturgy of the Church it enables us to attain the expectation of our hearts.

Jesus the God-Man is the High Priest of the human race who achieved true worship—perfect dialogue—with His heavenly Father. He did so by offering His life in the flesh (His "Physical Body," so to speak), and by dying and rising again. This is the Paschal Mystery.

Jesus did not relegate His actions just to the people of His time. He prolonged them for all succeeding ages through His Mystical Body, the Church. In this way, people of all times come in contact with Him, render fitting worship to the Father through the Holy Spirit, and obtain the saving benefits Jesus achieved once and for all.

The Church celebrates this Liturgy, this praise of God day and night on behalf of all. She prays for the world's salvation and fosters thanksgiving and praise to God. Every Sunday, she keeps the memory of our Lord's Paschal Mystery, and she continues to sanctify time and consecrate it to God by the Liturgical Year. She unfolds the whole Mystery of Christ—from the Incarnation and Birth to the Ascension, the day of Pentecost and even to the expectation of the Lord's Second Coming.

Through the Liturgy, we enter into the events of Christ's life. We encounter Christ—not in the flesh but in His Mysteries. And these have the power to sanctify us now as much as they had the power to sanctify those who met Jesus in the flesh on earth.

### Living Memorial of Christ

In ordinary human life, a living memory can be a great force for good or evil. The memory of a stirring stage performance can sustain an aging actor and move him to overcome present problems. The remembrance of a beloved parent can prompt a grown-up son or daughter to write a letter, begin an award, or utter a prayer for eternal peace. The power of memory is almost unfathomable.

The Liturgy may be termed the living memory of the Church, the community of witnesses to Christ. Through it, the Church recalls the Mysteries of Christ. In doing so, she is sustained by Christ the Son of God and enabled to span time. Thus, she feels the power of His mysteries in her members who are thereby sanctified and moved to act.

Over the course of centuries, the Church has structured this Memory into a yearly cycle commemorating one or other event of Christ's life. In traversing this liturgical year, the faithful are able to be more closely conformed to Christ by various other means as well—pious practices, instruction, prayer, and works of penance and mercy.

During Advent, we look forward with anticipation to a new coming of Christ in our lives, just as the people of old waited for the purifying coming of the Messiah. This is *His coming in mystery* to counterbalance *His coming in history* in the past and *His coming in glory* in the future.

During the Christmas Season, we rejoice over Christ's triple coming with all the benefits that it entails for us. We thank Him for obtaining salvation for us by His first coming; we ask Him to apply that salvation to us by this His second Coming; and we pray that He will complete that salvation for us at His third coming.

During the Lenten Season, we do penance and prepare to "die to self" with Christ. We diligently apply ourselves to eradicating all that is bad in us so that we may be "new persons" for Christ on Easter.

During the Easter Season, we are filled with joy in Christ's saving act and His glorification through His Resurrection. We celebrate the magnificent victory over sin and death that God has made possible for us in Christ.

During the Ordinary Time, we encounter Jesus in His ceaseless efforts to proclaim the Good News. We work to perfect His works in our day through the power of the Holy Spirit.

In this annual cycle, the Church also proclaims the Paschal Mystery achieved in the Saints who have suffered and been glorified with Christ. By keeping the memory of the Martyrs and all the Saints, she holds them up as examples drawing all to the Father through Christ, and through their merits she pleads for God's favors.

Hence, in the Liturgy we have a golden opportunity to encounter and get to know Christ in the best way. We will thus be able to praise the Father in spirit and in truth and we will take hold of the graces He attained for us. We will imbibe the necessary instruction to know and live our faith. Our slogan could be: "Jesus, yes—in the Church, yes."

Chapter 12
# THE HOLY SPIRIT: THE SOUL OF THE LITURGY

In the Acts of the Apostles, which is sometimes called "the Gospel of the Holy Spirit," there is an intriguing and perhaps prophetic passage. St. Paul is passing through Ephesus on his Second Missionary Journey when he comes upon some "disciples" of Christ. He asks if they have received the Holy Spirit on becoming believers. Their mystified reply is: "We have not even heard that there is a Holy Spirit!" (Ac 19:1-2).

Although the circumstances are different among today's believers, the Spirit remains the "unknown Person" of the Blessed Trinity. All Catholics have indeed heard of Him but few know anything about Him. Their reply might be: "We have heard that there is a Holy Spirit but we know little about who He is or what He does."

Such a declaration of ignorance could not be made, however, by anyone who pays close attention to the Liturgy. For the Liturgy is a school in which we learn the role played by the Holy Spirit in the Redemption, the great debt we owe to Him, and how we should honor and invoke Him.

This is merely another indication that the whole *liturgical cycle* is a reflection of the life of the Blessed Trinity, and its purpose is to enable us to share that life. Each of the three Persons work together to effect our salvation in accordance with that which characterizes each as Father, as Son, and as Holy Spirit.

The Father does not work alone but the Son works with Him, and the Holy Spirit works with both. Every operation going forth from the Father passes through the Son and is accomplished in the Holy Spirit.

This is what gives rise to the so-called Christological-Trinitarian activity of the sacred history of salvation: "Every good gift comes to us from the Father, through the medium of Jesus Christ His incarnate Son, in the presence of the Holy Spirit; and likewise, it is in the presence of the Holy

Spirit, through the medium of Jesus Christ the incarnate Son, that everything must return to the Father and be reunited with its end, the most Blessed Trinity."[46]

Thus, the Incarnation of the Second Person (Christ's Life, Death and Resurrection) is the work of the Holy Spirit. Jesus comes through the Holy Spirit. The action of the Spirit in Jesus is not an episodic or momentary one. It continues throughout His earthly life and existence. *The Spirit is the Spirit of Jesus.*

Everything Jesus said was said in the Spirit. All that He did was done in the Spirit. No one ever had the Spirit as Jesus did—the Spirit rested on Him (Is 61). He had the Spirit as part of Himself.

The Scriptures show God intervening more and more in His creation and giving Himself more and more so that human beings could live from Him. The Father conceives and sets in motion His plan of love. The Son comes to announce it with the words of a Man and to carry it out with a life and death of a Man. The Spirit gives us the power to love.

Thus, Jesus founds the Church: the Holy Spirit animates it. Jesus launches the mission; the Spirit authenticates it. Jesus institutes the Sacraments: the Spirit gives life to them. Jesus speaks: the Spirit makes His words understood.

Without the Spirit, God remains far away, Christ is locked into the past, the Gospel is only a dead letter, the Church is a mere organization, authority nothing more than domination. Mission becomes propaganda worship merely an evocation, and Christian action a morality of slavery.

### The Holy Spirit and the Liturgical Year

The liturgical year has been called "the masterpiece of the Holy Spirit." In the light of the Scriptures (inspired by the Holy Spirit), it sets forth the History of Salvation for us—and does so in such a way that we also become part of that History.[47]

The first phase or period of this History shows us the Father's careful and continuous cultivation of His chosen people—all completely geared toward the coming of His Son into the world. In this phase, the gift of the Spirit is a *personal* one. It is given to certain prominent persons (high priest, kings, and prophets) for the benefit of the community over which they preside.

In the second phase, the chief character is the Incarnate Word, Jesus

Christ. He took flesh to effect our salvation. He proclaimed His divine Message, accomplished our redemption by His cross and resurrection, and has been made a "life-giving spirit" who is a source of all grace and the primary cause of all spiritual life. For the humanity of Christ spiritualized and glorified in heaven gained the graces of the Holy Spirit (Whose fullness Jesus possesses) which flow into our souls.

The third phase is the life of the Church in which the Holy Spirit plays a leading part. It is the function of the Church, guided and vivified by the Holy Spirit, to bring us into contact with the Risen Lord and to ensure for us these graces which will enable us to die to sin and to live as true members of Christ.

In this respect, the Liturgy—the official worship of the Church and the principal instrument of the sanctification of souls by the Holy Spirit—plays its key part. In the celebration of this history of salvation through feasts, the Church inserts us into that history and enables the Holy Spirit to transform us into "other Christs."

The actions of our human bodies and the actions of the Holy Spirit combine to make the Liturgy not a mere sacramental dramatization of the History of Salvation. They make us more than simply spectators in a sacred drama. They render us *active participants* in the work of salvation in its third stage.

Just as the Spirit remains active throughout the first two phases of the History of Salvation, so is He active in the last phase. And He is active through the *liturgical memorial* of the salvific events.

## Worship in Spirit and in Truth

The Spirit is our link with the Father and the Son through the Liturgy. With the Holy Spirit the sacraments become the actions of the Risen Christ. St. John says that "what is born of the Spirit is spirit" (3:6). We become "spiritual" beings leading a "spiritual" life, the very life of the *Spirit of Love*, the "new life!"

Every Baptism is accomplished in the Spirit. As Jesus said to Nicodemus, "a person must be born again of water and the Spirit in order to enter the Kingdom of God" (Jn 3:5).

Confirmation is linked with Baptism. It confers the fullness of the Spirit received at Baptism.

The Sacrament of Penance was instituted on the evening of the Resurrection in an effusion of the Holy Spirit: "Receive the Holy Spirit: . . . sins will be forgiven" (Jn 20:22ff). The Spirit of Love is the universal reconciliation.

Matrimony is nothing more than the life of two human beings who pledge to share everything in such a way that their bodies have become "spiritual," temples of the Holy Spirit.

The Anointing of the Sick communicates to the sick the power of the Spirit who imparts to them life and love.

Holy Orders gives the grace of the Holy Spirit through the imposition of hands so that those who receive it take the place of Jesus Christ in a visible and evident manner.

Thus it is the Spirit who enables us to worship in Spirit and in truth (Jn 4:24). The whole Liturgy takes place in the Spirit. We give glory to the Father through the Son in the Holy Spirit, and gain sanctification for ourselves.

In the illumination of the Holy Spirit we see the true Light who enlightens everyone who comes into the world. In this light we see the glory of the only Son and we receive the knowledge of the Father.

Hence, the Spirit is the proper *place* (in a spiritual sense) for true worship. We offer worship *in* the Holy Spirit. The Spirit is the place of the Saints and the Saints are the proper place of the Spirit, offering themselves for the Spirit's indwelling and called His temple!

The Spirit is the eternal today in the life of the Church and Christians. The annual cycle of liturgical celebrations is not, as we have already mentioned, a simple evocation of the great events of the history of salvation of the mystery of the redemption. Those who take part in the Liturgy are enabled to take part in the Mystery as in the *today* of the mystery. And all this because we have been baptized, sanctified, and placed on the road to return through the Son in the Spirit toward the Father.

### The Holy Spirit in the Ordinary of the Mass

The Liturgy is a mystagogy, an entry into the mystery that unites heaven and earth through the fellowship of the Holy Spirit. The notion of memorial is applied only to the presence of Christ, since the notion of commemoration cannot be applied to any of the Divine Persons except the Second in His incarnation. Hence, the memorials of the Liturgy of the Church concern only commemoration of the economy of the Incarnate Word.

The Father is not the object of a memorial. The Church has no Feast of the Father or ikon of the Father. It is Christ who is the revelation and the perfect and adequate image of the Father: "Whoever sees Me sees the Father" (Jn 14:9). The Father is the term of the Church's memorials. They are addressed to Him so that He will remember His creation and in the creative memorial vivify and save His Church.

In the same way, the Holy Spirit is not the object of a memorial, either. Even the memorial of Pentecost is a commemoration of the completion of the *Paschal Mystery of Christ*—in which the Holy Spirit plays a part.

In time, Christians did come to appreciate the actions of the Holy Spirit through this memorial, and it became the object of a liturgical experience. For Jesus not only spoke *in the Spirit* (who was His Spirit and rested in Him in fullness); He also spoke *of* the Spirit.

Whenever the Church mentions the Holy Spirit in the Liturgy she does so in the Trinitarian formula: praise and glory to the Father through the Son in the Holy Spirit.

In the Ordinary of the Mass the Church names the Divine Persons in the order of their original differentiation: in the Sign of the Cross, the Greeting, the Gloria, the Creed, the Opening Prayers, and in the Eucharistic Prayers. The same is true in the Sacramental rites and the Liturgy of the Hours (in the Glory Be that concludes the Psalms and the Blessings before the Short Readings and the *Te Deum*).

Since the Holy Spirit is God and is active with Christ, the Church sometimes addresses Him directly just as she sometimes addresses Christ directly. She blesses *in* the Holy Spirit, and at the Gospel Acclamation for Pentecost she calls directly upon the Spirit—as she also does in the Sequence: "Come, Holy Spirit."

This honor is always rendered to the Spirit in His capacity as the perfecter of Christ's work and the Father's plan—to One Who refers all things to both. The Son, receiving all things from His Father, never ceased to refer all things to Him. In the same way, the Holy Spirit, receiving all from the Father and the Son, never ceases to be a witness to them and to be our indispensable link with them. This is how the Church always presents Him in the Opening *Prayer*.

## The Holy Spirit in the Eucharistic Prayer

The purpose of Christ's resurrection and ascension was not to take Him away from His disciples but to make Him present to them in a new way. He was to live on *in them*. This is the goal of the Eucharist in our respect.

This is carried out by the Holy Spirit in the Eucharist, by realizing the fruits of the Eucharist in the faithful but also by being intimately bound up with the transformation of the bread and wine into the Body and Blood of Christ. This enables Him to "spiritualize" those participating in the Eucharist.

This "spiritualizing" involves two aspects. The Holy Spirit makes the Body and Blood of Christ, in a sense, capable of achieving its saving effects in the faithful, and He works in the hearts of the faithful to open them up to the actions of the sacramental body and blood of the Lord.

This in no way means that the Holy Spirit *replaces* Christ in the Eucharist. The Eucharist is always and everywhere an action of the Risen Lord and of His Spirit. It is the Risen Lord exercising His lordship in the Spirit—or the Spirit of the Lord at work.

What we have just sketched is the question of the *Epiclesis*, which has caused rivers of ink to flow over the centuries between the Eastern and the Western Church. This word means *invocation* but technically refers to an invocation pronounced after the Institution Narrative asking that the Holy Spirit may sanctify the offerings.

It stems from our human approach to God. We ask God for something that *we know will be done* because it is *Christ in His Spirit* who is doing it. But since we *pray in time* we cannot put all of this in its true sequence.

The Roman Canon (Eucharistic Prayer I) had an implicit Epiclesis before the Consecration (*Hanc igitur*) and an explicit one after it (*Supplices*). The new Eucharistic Prayers have two Epicleses, one before and one after the Consecration, and both are a petition to the Father for the gift of the Spirit.

The first Epiclesis in all three cases asks for the Consecration. These are accompanied by the imposition of hands, a traditional sign of the Spirit.

We ask for the Spirit because the Consecration is a prolongation or a consequence of the Incarnation, and the Incarnation was accomplished by the action of the Holy Spirit. Similarly, the Eucharist is a sanctification, and sanctification is the work of the Holy Spirit.

The second Epiclesis comes after the Consecration and asks that this (the Consecration) be accomplished. It asks that in his Eucharist Christ may become present not merely to assure His presence among us, for that is already realized by other means. It asks for His substantial and personal presence to be effected under the forms of bread and wine, which we can eat and drink, so that it may become the *means of our union with Him*.

This is, in the words of the Second Vatican Council, the fruit of every

Mass. Thus, the role of the Holy Spirit in the Eucharistic Prayer and in the Epiclesis can underline for us the fact that God realizes the Eucharist *for* the assembly, especially the participating assembly.

The transformation of the gifts into the Body and Blood of Christ finds its meaning and purpose in the sanctification of the assembled faithful. This sanctification should take place through the reception of the gifts. God realizes the bodily Presence of Christ in the Eucharist for the assembly, especially a community assembly.

Similarly, God realizes the Eucharist through the *believing* assembly. God merely takes the initiative. He is doubtless free and sovereign in realizing the Eucharist. Yet the Church (represented by the assembly) plays a role in the realization of the sacrament—no matter how subordinate that role is. Without the faith of the Church, there is no sacrament.

The Eucharist involves both Christ present and offering himself to his Church and the Church accepting and responding to this offer *in faith*. Also involved is an invitation to each individual in the assembly personally to share in Christ's presence and thus have it attain the goal for which it was instituted.

Finally, the assembly has a share in the realization of this Eucharist only as a *praying* assembly. The assembly is aware that it cannot force God to realize the Eucharist. It therefore trusts Him to do so. It *prays* that He will make the Eucharist realized here and now for this assembly.

## The Twofold Presence of the Holy Spirit

Theologians distinguish two presences of the Holy Spirit in the Church, in the sacraments and in the Eucharist. These two presences are (1) functional and (2) personal.

The Event of Pentecost is not limited to a "spiritual" presence of the glorified Lord in His Church. It also signifies the coming of the "economy of the Holy Spirit." This means the personal presence of the consoler, the spirit of truth whom the Father sends in the Name of Jesus (Jn 14:26), and whom Jesus Himself sends from the Father (Jn 15:26).

The coming of the Holy Spirit does not have a subordinate and *functional* character with respect to the work of Christ. The Spirit is *present in person* and He acts in the Church, in rendering this Church and her human members conformed to Christ.

The "economy of the Holy Spirit" and the "economy of the Son" are in no way opposed to one another. The time of the Spirit does not succeed the time of Christ but constitutes its completion, plenitude, and manifestation.

The Church is in the time of Pentecost but the Spirit of Pentecost is the agent of the permanent presence of the Lord in His Church and of the access to and intimacy with the Father as well as the fruit and the personal gift of Christ—risen and ascended to the Father's right hand.

It is important not to confuse these two aspects of Pentecost and consequently of the whole sacramental and Eucharistic nature of the Church. On the one hand, the Holy Spirit bears witness to Christ, enabling us to invoke Christ, rendering Christ present, and conforming us to Him. On the other hand, Christ in turn sends us the Holy Spirit, praying to the Father for the gifts of the Spirit for us.

There is thus a twofold perspective in the Eucharist. Or to put it another way there are two Epicletic orientations in the Eucharist. The first orientation is christological. By her worship the Church is turned toward Christ, and she addresses herself to Him in her public or private prayer (for example, the Kyrie, the Maranatha—"Come, Lord Jesus"—the Hosanna, even the Trisagion—"Holy, holy, holy").

These are liturgical approaches to Christ that can be made only in the Holy Spirit. This results from the inspiration of the Holy Spirit ever since Pentecost which renews the Church and renders her capable of invoking Christ: waiting for Him, recognizing and confessing Him, and finally proclaiming Him. It is only through the Holy Spirit that the Church can confess Christ Jesus as Lord (1 Cor 12:13).

The second orientation is pneumatological in its object. Through it the Church asks the Father for the gift of the Holy Spirit. This is founded in the data of the New Testament, in particular in the Johannine writings reproducing Christ's Farewell to His disciples. Christ promises that He will pray to the Father and this prayer will be an Epiclesis—it will ask for the Holy Spirit: "I will ask the Father, and He will send you another Advocate" (Jn 14:16).

In turn, this request for the Holy Spirit is a permanent Epiclesis of the Church and it can only be done in Christ, through Christ, and with Christ, since the Church harmonizes her prayer with the permanent heavenly prayer of the Christ who is exalted at the Father's right hand. The whole Liturgy must be seen in the perspective of Christ's Ascension, of His seating at the right hand of the Father, and of His heavenly intercession which is the Epiclesis of the Father par excellence, the perspective in which the Church subsists in her earthly prayer.

## The Fellowship of the Holy Spirit

The role of the Holy Spirit is not limited in the Eucharist to working the "real Presence" of Christ in the consecrated elements. The consecrating and sanctifying acts of the Holy Spirit cannot be limited to an Epicletic formula but extend to the whole Eucharistic Action.

Catholic tradition has come up with a term to express the reality of the transformation of the faithful, and to show the finality of the transformation of the elements, for the sanctification of the faithful by the Holy Spirit who acts in matter and in the human heart. This term is "fellowship of the Holy Spirit."

It flows from the theology of St. Paul: "May the grace of our Lord Jesus Christ, the love of God the Father, and the *fellowship* of the Holy Spirit be with you" (2 Cor 13:13). This formula expresses the consubstantiality of the Holy Spirit with the Father and the Son; in accord with the principle of the economy of the Holy Spirit, it affirms His full divinity while not using the word God. It applies the notion of the "fellowship of the Holy Spirit" to the whole Providence of the Holy Spirit over the Angels, people, and all creation. This fellowship signifies a real participation of human beings or Angels or creation in the life of God, and is the fruit of the Eucharist: in the words of an Epiclesis found in the Eastern Liturgy, "so that they may become for those who receive [the Body and Blood] purification of soul, remission of sins, fellowship of Your Holy Spirit, Fullness of the Kingdom of Heaven, trust in You, and not judgment or condemnation."

At Pentecost the Church received the Holy Spirit after Christ had ascended to heaven; now she receives the gifts of the Holy Spirit after the offerings have been accepted at the heavenly altar. God who has accepted these gifts sends us in return the Holy Spirit as He promised: for the Mediator is the same, today as always, and it is also the same Holy Spirit.

It is this same reality of the Holy Spirit that introduces us into the communion of the trinitarian life. One of the prayers after communion of the Eastern Liturgy says: "We have seen the true light, we have received the Holy Spirit, we have found the true Father by adoring the indivisible Trinity: it is this which has saved us!"

Christians are called to realize everywhere the "liturgical" being that we have become through the Spirit, constantly ministering in Christ before the Father, creating new relations between human beings and creation.

The Divine Liturgy is accomplished in public before the eyes of all and yet secretly too, just as Christ was seen but not always recognized. By precepts of Christ are easier for us to carry out, and His yoke becomes light.

Leaving the church, we will look upon all others as brothers and sisters in Christ. In our daily work, study, or leisure, we will retain in ourselves a supernatural love for others. We will be one in the unity of the Holy Spirit.

The Spirit thus enables the faithful to fulfill our true role, the liturgical role for which we have been created—for the glory of God. St. Irenaeus said: "The glory of God is a living person; or the life of a person is the vision of God."[48]

This reveals the Old Testament notion that among human beings worship is a task inherent to their proper vocation. The sense of worship rendered by people created to the image of God whose glory they reflect is tied to their place in the universe. They are spokespersons of creation. Henceforth, human nature, assumed into the economy of the Incarnation participates in the eternal acts of the Son Who has risen and is seated at the right hand of the Father forever.

This worship communicates the lively sense of the communion of saints, of the intercommunion of heaven and earth. The liturgical life is in all participating actively in the sacred ceremonies, our souls are elevated, the this a living and existential interpretation of the Scriptures. Through the medium of the Holy Spirit, the liturgical time is a participation in the eternity of God.

The Church in its essential catholicity and holiness becomes the revealer of the world—of this world. All whom the Church takes hold of are led, once converted to Jesus Christ, in a vast liturgy for which the whole world has been created (Gn 1:-2:4). Human life has no sense except a liturgical one—and this extends not only to all human life but also to all of creation.

We are living in the era of the Holy Spirit, which is that of the "last hour." We must never sadden the Spirit and still less extinguish that same Spirit: "Build yourselves up in your most holy faith and pray in the Holy Spirit. Keep yourselves in God's love as you wait for the coming or our Lord Jesus Christ to bring you to eternal life" (Jude 20-22).

Chapter 13
# MARY IN THE LITURGY: A SURE GUIDE TO TRUE MARIAN DEVOTION

In an Apostolic Exhortation Pope Paul VI indicated that the devotees of the Blessed Virgin Mary had nothing to fear from the liturgical renewal:
> We should not fear that the Liturgical Renewal . . . can work to the detriment of the singular devotion owed to the Blessed Virgin Mary because of her prerogatives, among which the dignity of *Mother of God* is paramount. Nor should we fear the opposite—that the increase of devotion, whether Liturgical or private, will overshadow or diminish the cult of adoration rendered to the Incarnate Word as well as to the Father and the Son.[49]

In the decade and a half that has intervened, these words have proven to be prophetic. Devotion to Mary has not only survived but actually flourished. At the same time, the devotion is wholly oriented toward increasing devotion to the Persons of the Trinity.

The devotion to Mary takes its origin and expression from Christ, finds its complete expression in Christ, and leads through Christ in the Spirit to the Father! This devotion necessarily reflects God's redemptive plan, in which a special form of veneration is appropriate to the singular place which Mary occupies in that plan.

Devotion is rendered to Mary because she is the *chosen Daughter of the Father, faithful Spouse of the Spirit, and devoted Mother of the Son.* Her prerogatives flow from these qualities and make her the loving *Mother of the Church* as well as the closest imitator of Christ and thus model of the faithful.

As the Liturgy honors Mary over the course of a year the Mysteries of Christ become present to us in their relationship with her. We must undertake a particular devotion to the Blessed Mother if we want to insure that the historico-spiritual event for which we prepare will attain its true purposes.

## LITURGY—OUR SCHOOL OF FAITH

### The Cult of Mary—Hyperdulia

Theologians give a special name to the cult rendered to Mary by the Church—it is termed *hyperdulia*. It is infinitely inferior to the worship rendered to God alone—which is termed *latria*. Yet it is far above the veneration accorded to Saints—which is known as *dulia*. Veneration for Mary is completely distinctive.

The early Christians made natural use of the salutations of the Angel Gabriel and Elizabeth recorded in the Gospel: "Hail Mary, full of grace, the Lord is with you"; and "Blessed are you among women and blessed is the fruit of your womb." She was also venerated as the holy one, the Blessed Virgin, and the all-holy.

Beginning with the 4th century, we find two forms of veneration accorded to the Blessed Virgin: the "memory of the Blessed Virgin Mary, Mother of God" in the Roman Canon of the Mass and the direct recourse to her intercession in accord with the popular prayer *Sub tuum* ("Under your protection we fly, O holy Mother of God. Despise not our petitions in our necessities, but deliver us always from all dangers, O glorious and blessed Virgin").

The Church also made early use of the Canticle of the *Magnificat* (uttered by Mary in Luke's Gospel) to express its own worship of praise to the Father through the Son in the Spirit.

In time the Marian liturgical feasts arose out of different circumstances owing to four main sources: (1) Some feasts emerged from the theme of Christ's birth: Maternity of Mary, the Annunciation, and the Presentation of the Lord. (2) Other feasts originated from the dedication of basilicas erected at Jerusalem: Birth of Mary, Presentation of Mary, and Assumption of the Holy Mother of God. (3) Still other feasts arose from a better understanding of the Faith, nourished by reflection on the Gospel: Immaculate Conception, Visitation, and Sorrows of Mary. (4) Finally, some modern feasts consecrated particular devotions to Mary: Queenship of Mary, Immaculate Heart of Mary and Our Lady of the Rosary; while others recalled important places of Marian devotion: Our Lady of Lourdes, Our Lady of Mount Carmel, Saint Mary Major, and in the United States, Our Lady of Guadalupe.

In the Offices of the Blessed Virgin as well as in the spiritual interpretation of the Psalms or the Book of Revelation, the Church identifies herself with Mary in some way. She sees in Mary the Daughter of Zion, the Mother

## Mary in the Liturgy: A Sure Guide to True Marian Devotion

of nations, the Bride, the Woman clothed with the Sun, Jerusalem, and the Temple—all figures of the Church herself.

At the basis of the liturgical cult of Mary there is an awareness of the role played by the Blessed Virgin in the work of salvation and in the very life of the Church, and an experience of communion in the Mystery of Christ. Mary holds a primary place in this mystery because of the close bond that ties her to her Son, as Mother of God, and to the Church herself as most eminent member and Mother in the Spirit.

The Church finds in Mary the most perfect expression and the exemplar of the worship in Spirit and in truth which she must render to God when she celebrates the Divine Mysteries. We might say that the entire Liturgy is Marian even if it is not always explicit.

### Three Principal Forms of Marian Devotion

The Church makes room for Mary in her public prayer to God (1) by stressing Mary's acceptance of the Word of God or what the Scriptures tell us on the subject, (2) by identifying with Mary in the offering of the Sacrifice of Christ on the Cross, or (3) by indirectly having recourse to her intercession in heaven.

The perfect type of this first form is found in the Preface of the Blessed Virgin Mary. There are also the mentions of the memory of the Blessed Virgin in the Ordinary of the Mass, in the Creed, in a few Prefaces, and in the new Eucharistic Prayers.

The liturgical seasons of Advent and Christmas give a prominent place to Mary both in the Readings and in the texts of the Mass or Office.

Certain feasts of the Liturgical Calendar like the Presentation and the Annunciation are just as much feasts of our Lord as they are feasts of Mary. The same is true of the Motherhood of Mary. The Blessed Virgin is also mentioned in the formulary of a certain number of other feasts in addition to those of Christmas and Epiphany and the Holy Family: St. Joseph (March 19 and May 1) and St. Joachim and Ann (July 26).

Finally, Mary is mentioned in Ritual Masses: Consecration of Virgins, Religious Profession, Christian Initiation, Funerals of Children, and Migrants as well as a certain number of Sunday and Weekday Readings (15 new Readings in addition to the Readings for the Common of the Blessed Virgin).

The Church honors Mary by blessing the Lord for allowing her to take part in the major events of the life of her Son, as they are reported to us in the Gospel and by tradition. She also praises the Lord for granting the particular graces that prepared Mary for her mission and for the reward He granted her both in soul and in body as well as for a certain number of events in the life of the people of God in which the action of Mary was made manifest in a more particular fashion. These provide the occasion for having recourse to Mary's intercession so as to be able to imitate her example or benefit from her protection.

This is where the Marian feasts properly so-called come in together with the Common of the Dedication of the Blessed Virgin. Finally, there is the special Solemn Blessing for feasts of Mary which utilizes the first two forms of Marian Devotion mentioned here.

In prayer to Mary, the Church addresses herself directly no longer to God but to Mary herself in order to praise and honor her, in the fashion of the Gospel formulas of praise already mentioned and also to have direct recourse to her intercession.

This type of devotion is found beginning with the 9th century in Hymns (*Ave Maris Stella*—Hail, Star of the Sea) and Anthems (*Salve Regina*—Hail, Holy Queen) dedicated to Mary as well as in later Prose like the *Stabat Mater*—The Mother Stood by [the Cross] and, toward the 12th century, in the *Confiteor* (I Confess) at Mass.

In this last form, we can properly speak of a "special place of Mary in the liturgical worship of the Church." The formulas of Marian feasts also present Gospel Acclamations or Canticles that are directly addressed to Mary.

Prayer addressed directly to Mary has God as its last term; it is not an end in itself. Thus, it is the Father who receives honor and praise for the wisdom of His designs manifested in Mary. Through the honor tendered to Mary it is Christ her Son who is better known and loved. It is the action of the Spirit in Mary and in the Church that is acknowledged and proclaimed.

### Presence of Mary in the Celebration of the Eucharist

Mary cooperated in a singular way in the Savior's work of restoring supernatural grace to souls—she is a mother to us in the order of grace. By reason of this close connection with Christ and us, Mary could not be absent from our celebration of the Eucharist.

We must not see her presence there as the presence of Christ. The consecration effects the Real Presence of the Christ of Glory in the act of His Sacrifice under the appearances of bread and wine, with His body and blood, soul and divinity. Nothing of the kind is true in Mary's humanity. Yet the Presence of Jesus brings with it in some way the presence of His Mother.

The Christ who becomes present on the altar is the same Christ who took from Mary His body and blood of the Eucharistic Sacrifice which are given as nourishment to us. The reality of the Word made flesh can be perceived only in its twofold relation of Son: the one according to which He is eternally engendered by the Father and the one according to which He was begotten in time by Mary.

Hence, our faith in the Eucharistic Christ includes a background reference to His Mother according to the flesh: *Ave verum Corpus natum de Maria*—Hail true Body born of the Virgin Mary!

In addition, the real action that Christ exercises in the Eucharist brings with it the presence of those on whom His action is exercised, and whom He gathers together through it. This action, which transcends the limits of time and space, concerns in the first place Mary.

Inasmuch as she is the beneficiary, the first fruit of the Redemption, the first and perfect Christian, Mary lives in the glory of the life of her Son, because she does not cease to receive it from Him. This is in virtue of the unique and ever active offering by which He has "rendered perfect forever those whom He sanctifies" (Heb 10:14). Wherever Christ's Sacrifice is, there too is Mary, like the stream that cannot be cut off from its source.

Associated with the work of salvation, Mary retains her special place in God's plan of redemption. Her presence at the Cross is the guarantee of an ever active presence in the Eucharist of her Son. She can only exercise her mediation "interiorly" to the salvific action of Jesus but wherever this action is, there too is the action of Mary!

Thus, at every Liturgical Celebration, Mary the Mother of God is with us—as our Model, our Intercessor, and our Mother. And she is even more each of these things in the Marian celebrations. We should have frequent recourse to her and increase our devotion to her.

Each Marian liturgical celebration is also intended to give us a better understanding of Mary's part in our salvation, a true catechesis of Mary. A clear example of this is found in one of the latest Marian Liturgical Rites issued by the Church—the Rite for Crowning an Image of the Blessed Virgin Mary.

## A Little Summa of Marian Theology

On March 25, 1981 the Congregation for the Sacraments and Divine Worship promulgated the *Ordo coronandi imaginem beatae Mariae Virginis* (The Rite for Crowning an Image of the Blessed Virgin Mary). This new rite takes the place of the one that had been inserted in the *Roman Pontifical* in the 19th century in response to the Church's devotion to Mary from the earliest ages. It can be celebrated by a bishop or a priest in his absence.

The ceremony of Mary's crowning can now take place in three types of liturgical services: (1) during the celebration of the Eucharist; (2) during Evening Prayer of the Liturgy of the Hours: and (3) during a Liturgy of the Word.

By this action the Church provided us with a beautiful and liturgical way of honoring the Queen of heaven and increasing devotion to her. At the same time, the Church also put a precious teaching tool in the hands of all who are entrusted with handing on the Catholic Faith to others.

The texts of this new rite constitute a golden treasury of ideas and insights for inculcating devotion to Mary our Queen and communicating the genuine meaning of her queenship. Indeed, the rite can be termed a little summa of Marian theology.

In line with the approach of all the revised liturgical texts, the Church strives to make the texts of this rite speak to the people of today in terms that they will understand. For the most part the texts are taken from the Bible as God's perennial Word, the Documents of the Second Vatican Council with its pastoral orientation and emphasis on contemporary Catholic culture, and previous Liturgical Texts that have become part of the Tradition of the Church.

The rite has not yet been promulgated in its English dress for official liturgical purposes but there is little doubt that it could easily be adapted for use at a May crowning which is traditional in some Catholic schools. It could also be combed for profitable homiletic material for May devotions.[50]

## Mary's Queenship in a Secular Society

This rite renders a service to Catholics by providing almost a textbook sample of how true devotion to Mary can be attained even in Marian themes that would seem to be too difficult to reconcile with modern thought.

# Mary in the Liturgy: A Sure Guide to True Marian Devotion    113

In the recent past the objection was raised that terms and symbols like queen and crown pertained to a time gone by, one permeated by political and cultural conceptions that were no longer in vogue. Hence, these terms should not be used in the Liturgy, for they would be meaningless to present-day Catholics or even drive them away from the desired teaching.

Another objection was that the whole rite of crowning could foster a triumphalist view—the type of Marian piety that focused almost exclusively on the greatness of Mary and obscured the profile of her given us by the Gospel. Such a view not only presents us with solely half a picture of the real Mary but also distorts Catholic beliefs about Mary and hinders ecumenical efforts.

The Church's Liturgy is ideally constituted to resolve these two problems. For it is intimately connected with the Word of God, takes full account of Tradition, listens intently to the Magisterium, diligently eschews polemics and all spirit of divisiveness, possesses a wonderful capacity for synthesis and a natural bent for contemplation and is endowed with wide experience in grappling with theological themes for the major Seasons. In addition the Liturgy is imbued with an inexhaustible supply of patience, a deep love for graciousness and beauty and is in tune with the voices of the people.

As far as the terms queen and crown are concerned, a few years ago they may indeed have seemed to be anachronistic. Today in the wake of a whole world's attentiveness to the marriage of a future king of England, such a view can only be characterized as academic. Furthermore, there is a decided swing back to the natural as a result of the whole ecological movement. Words, images, and symbols taken from the world of nature are regaining currency. Even the field of technology is making more use of simple words and images to communicate its most sophisticated ideas and products.

## Mary's Queenship in Modern Church Documents

The latest documents of the Church have not shrunk from using such "anachronistic" terms to communicate spiritual realities and moral values. The Second Vatican Council, for example, vigorously affirmed Mary's Queenship without apology and without any fear of the teaching being distorted by its hearers:

Finally, the Immaculate Virgin, preserved free from all guilt of original sin, on the completion of her earthly sojourn, was taken up body and soul into heavenly glory, *and exalted by the Lord as Queen of the universe*, that she might be more fully conformed to her Son, the Lord of lords and the conqueror of sin and death.[51]

The Post-conciliar Liturgy has also continued to use the term king with reference to Christ and queen with reference to Mary. In the Liturgy of the Hours, for example, we encounter significant expressions of Mary's Queenship in the Latin hymns for Morning Prayer, Daytime Prayer, and Evening Prayer in the Office for the Birth of Mary (Sept. 8).

Furthermore, the Solemnity of the Assumption constitutes the fullest celebration of Mary's Queenship. The Feast of the Queenship of Mary assigned to August 22 appears as a "festive prolongation" of the Assumption, as a special contemplation of "her who seated beside the King of the ages shines forth as Queen and intercedes as Mother."[52]

Finally, the well-known Puebla Document of the Third General Conference of the Latin American Episcopate (1979) characterizes the Blessed Virgin as the "maternal Queen . . . who now reigns and intercedes for human beings still sojourning in history . . . as the Queen of our various countries and the entire continent."[53]

This last testimony is particularly important. It is the expression not only of the largest Episcopal Conference of the Church but also of the people who were listened to by the bishops. The main texts were subjected to sharp debate and they come from a continent in which there is no queen in the social and political sphere.

### Mary's Queenship in the New Rite

The new rite provides a *biblical basis* for Christ's kingship and Mary's queenship. It roots both in the Paschal Mystery, Christ's self-offering, death, and resurrection-ascension. And this is itself ultimately rooted in our Lord's words about reaching glory through humility and about the primacy of love and service.

The prayer before the crowning accentuates the fact that in the plan of God Christ's abasement is followed by His exaltation at the Father's right hand. This Paschal Mystery (abasement-exaltation) is *prolonged in the members of Christ*, especially Mary His Mother and perfect follower. The event of the Assumption is the Virgin's Passover, the moment of her final configuration to the risen Christ:

## Mary in the Liturgy: A Sure Guide to True Marian Devotion

The Blessed Virgin Mary wanted to be called Your handmaid.
She was chosen as the Mother of the Redeemer
and the real Mother of all the living.
Now she is exalted over the choirs of angels
and reigning in glory with her Son.
She offers prayers for all human beings,
as the Advocate of grace and the Queen of mercy.

The prayer concludes with a request that the faithful who participate in the rite will live in the light of the Paschal Mystery:

Help them to deny themselves
and lose their own lives
in order to gain the souls of their brothers and sisters.
Let them follow the modest things on earth
and reach the heights in heaven
where You reward Your faithful servants
with the crown of life.

The new rite is festive and glorious yet it also initiates an attitude that is altogether different. What it comes down to is the practical application of one of the most paradoxical aspects of the Divine way of acting: God does not judge according to appearances (1 S 16:7). He does not kowtow to the rich and the world rulers. To use Mary's words, He confounds the proud in their inmost thoughts, deposes the mighty from their thrones, and raises the lowly to high places (Lk 1:51f).

Mary's Queenship stems from her humility and abasement. Thus, the faithful are urged to imitate her life of lowliness which is a following of Christ's life. When we see Mary crowned, we must also keep in mind the modest character of her life on earth: the humble home of Nazareth where she worked out her lowliness in union with God the Father and the Word Who became flesh in her upon her declaration of servanthood (Lk 1:38); the city of Judah (Lk 1:39) where she visited Elizabeth and uttered her *Magnificat* that gave forth the spirituality of the poor of Yahweh; and Calvary where she stood firm before the final abasement of her Son as "*He drew all things to Himself*" (Jn 12:32).

Therefore, it becomes clear to the faithful who truly listen to the liturgical texts that the God who has exalted Mary of Nazareth—a lowly and poor woman, faithful to His Word—will also exalt all those who in our day are persecuted and humiliated because of their fidelity to the Gospel.

Mary's Queenship is a Queenship not of pomp and power but of *love and service* in the same way that Christ's Kingdom is described by the

Gospel: "My Kingdom does not belong to this world" (Jn 18:36); "the Son of Man has come not to be served by others but to serve, to give His own life as a ransom for the many" (Mt 20:28).

The service of the Blessed Mother during her life on earth is full of adherence to God's plan and total dedication to the Son and His saving work:

> On earth Mary was always humble,
> the handmaid of the Lord.
> She devoted herself totally
> to her Son and His work.
> With Him and under Him
> she served the Mystery of the Redemption.

Assumed into heaven, she continues to manifest this love and service as a *minister of piety* by interceding with God for us so that all her children may attain salvation.

The rite goes on to remind us that we are all destined to reign with Christ, in accord with the words of St. Paul: "If we have died with Him, we shall also live with Him; if we hold out to the end, we shall also reign with Him" (2 Tm 2:11f). But it stresses that the path to this royalty for us is the same as it was for Christ and Mary—*through love and service*.

This festive rite of Mary's crowning is more than just an act of devotion to Mary. It constitutes an expressive celebration of the Christian commitment. Through the close connection between rite and life, the faithful who crown an image of Mary are the disciples who seriously take on the commandment to love and bind themselves to serve their brothers and sisters of the human family to the very loss of their own self.

### The Meaning of Mary's Queenship

The rite thus makes the reasons for Mary's Queenship crystal clear. She deserves to be Queen because she is: (1) the Mother of the Son of God and the Messianic King; (2) the loving Associate of the Redeemer; (3) the perfect follower (or disciple) of Christ; and (4) the most excellent member of the Church.

1) Mary is Queen because she is Mother of the Word Incarnate; because she "brought forth a Son Who at the very moment of His conception was—by virtue of the hypostatic union of the human nature with the Word—even as man King and Lord of all things."[54] And in this Incarnate

## Mary in the Liturgy: A Sure Guide to True Marian Devotion 117

Word "everything in heaven and on earth was created, things visible and things invisible, whether thrones or dominations, principalities or powers" (Col 1:16).

Mary is Queen also because she is the Mother of the Messianic King; because she bore a Son about whom the Angel said: "Great will be His dignity and He will be called Son of the Most High. The Lord God will give Him the throne of David His father. He will rule over the house of Judah forever and His reign will be without end" (Lk 1:32f). The rite adds Elizabeth's salutation to Mary: "Who am I that the Mother of my Lord should come to me?" as another Biblical indication of Mary's Queenship.

2) The Blessed Virgin is Queen because she was associated wholeheartedly with Christ the Redeemer. "By an eternal plan of God, the Blessed Virgin . . . is the new Eve and she played a great part in the work of salvation by which Christ Jesus, the new Adam, redeemed us and purchased us for Himself not with corruptible gold or silver but with His Precious Blood (1 P 1:18f) and made us into a Kingdom for our God (Rv 5:15)."

3) Mary is Queen because she was the perfect follower or disciple of Christ. This is a new theme and comes from the Book of Revelation (via Vatican II): "Remain faithful until death and I will give you the crown of life . . . . I will give the victor the right to sit with Me on the throne as I Myself won the victory and took My seat beside My Father on His throne" (Rv 2:10; 3:21).

In numbers 55-59 of the *Constitution on the Church*, Vatican II spelled out the role of the Blessed Virgin in the economy of salvation. The conciliar text makes it clear that Mary was totally united with her Son "in the work of salvation . . . from the time of Christ's virginal conception to His Death." The rite incorporates this theme in a concise and concrete fashion:

Mary consented to the Divine plan
and advanced in the journey of faith.
She heard and kept the Word of God
and faithfully preserved her union with the Son
even to the Cross.
She then persevered in prayer together with the Church
and became proficient in the love of God.

4) Mary is also the "most excellent member of the Church," according to a felicitous phrase of the Council.[55] She is "blest among women" (Lk 1:42) and holds a preeminent place in the Communion of Saints for a twofold reason: her mission and her holiness.

Mary stands out in the chosen race, priestly people, and holy nation which is the Church because of the *singular mission* given her with regard to Christ and all members of His Mystical Body, and because of her copious virtues and fullness of grace. Therefore, she deserves to be called the Lady of human beings and angels and the Queen of all Saints.

Mary's glory reverberates even outside the Church. She is the daughter of Adam and our Lady. She is thus not only the joy of Israel and the splendor of the Church, but also the glory of the entire human race.

The rite does not spell out this last aspect but it can easily be filled in by the section in the Apostolic Exhortation of Paul VI on *Devotion to Mary*[56] which shows Mary as a type of the modern woman. Thus, the modern woman, anxious to participate with decision-making power in the affairs of the country, can concentrate on Mary who, taken into dialogue with God, gives her active and responsible consent. Mary does so not to some passing problem but to an event of world importance—the Incarnation.

The modern woman can appreciate that Mary's choice of the state of virginity was not a rejection of any of the values of the married state. It was, in keeping with the Divine plan, a courageous choice which she made in order to consecrate herself totally to the love of God.

The modern woman can note with pleasant surprise that Mary, while completely devoted to the will of God, was far from being a timidly submissive woman or one whose piety was repellent to others. She was rather a woman who did not hesitate to proclaim that God vindicates the humble and the oppressed while He removes the powerful of this world from their privileged positions (see Lk 1:53f).

The modern woman can recognize in Mary, who stands out among the poor and humble of the Lord, a woman of strength, who experienced poverty and suffering, flight and exile (see Mt 2:13-23).

### A New Litany—A Paean to Mary's Queenship

One of the most innovative features of the rite is a new Litany of the Blessed Virgin which is especially suitable to be prayed and meditated upon. It has been drawn up with modern people in mind and includes well-known *traditional elements* that appeal to us at once: the opening threefold invocation, *Lord, have mercy*; the beloved response, *pray for us*; the first three invocations to Mary, *Holy Mary, Holy Mother of God,* Holy

## Mary in the Liturgy: A Sure Guide to True Marian Devotion 119

Virgin of Virgins; and the triple imploration of the *Lamb of God* at the end.

The essence of this litany rests in its emphasis on Mary's queenship. It defines the *specific area* of her queenship; she is Queen of *charity* because she excels in charity (a necessity for all followers of Jesus). She wields her influence over the faithful so that they may attain charity. And as *Queen of charity* she is also *Queen of mercy* and *Queen of peace*, for mercy and peace flow from charity.

The litany goes on to set forth the *groups* (angelical, Old Testament, and New Testament) over whom Mary presides because of the depth of her service and the purity of her love. These are: *Angels, Prophets, Apostles, Martyrs, Confessors, Virgins,* and *All Saints*. The *boundaries* of Mary's kingdom are delineated and they are the same as those of her Son's kingdom: she is Queen of *the world*, of *heaven*, and of *the universe*.

This modern and inspiring litany is based on the finest sources and they are evident when we utter the invocations: (a) Sacred Scripture: *Virgin Daughter of Zion*; *Handmaid of the Lord*; *Woman crowned with the stars*. (b) Formulas of Previous Litanies: the first three invocations are from the Litany of the Saints; the group of invocations from *Queen of Angels* to *Queen conceived without original sin* are from the Litany of Loreto. (c) Documents of Vatican II: *Most excellent fruit of the Redemption*;[57] *Queen of the universe* and *Associate of the Redeemer*;[58] (d) Liturgical Texts: *Advocate of grace* (Preface for Dec. 8), *Queen of heaven, Queen of the world,* and *Queen of mercy*.

There is little doubt that this new rite lends itself to many uses for the benefit of both priests and people. The themes in the rite are in fact very modern. The rite is suffused with Scripture, solid Catholic teaching, and contemporary emphases. All that is required to appreciate its truth and beauty is a little patience and an open mind. The texts will do the rest. They will imbue the hearers with love and admiration for Mary and for her Divine Son, and insure that they will go *to Jesus through Mary*.

Chapter 14

# THE LITURGICAL CELEBRATIONS OF THE SAINTS

We do not know the precise etymology of the word *saint*. In Hebrew the word that corresponds to it is *qadosh*, which means "to be cut off or separated from." In Greek the corresponding word is *haghion*, with the same meaning.

The reality which this word is intended to signify is first and foremost God—He is the Saint par excellence: "I, the Lord, your God, am holy" (Lv 19:2). To be holy, in this case, signifies to be powerful, perfect, separated from all imperfection and evil. The divine holiness or sanctity includes all that God possesses of richness and life, power and goodness.

God does not want to keep this holiness to Himself. He desires to communicate it to human beings and have them share it with him. Thus, he loves to show forth His holiness: "I will sanctify My great Name, which has been dishonored among the nations, and profaned by you in their midst. Then the nations shall know that I am the Lord, when I will show My sanctity in you before their eyes" (Ez 36:23).

For, God, to show forth His holiness means to free His people, to save them from political slavery and purify them from sin. The Holy One of Israel who has freed His people is the Creator of the whole world, the Lord of peoples (Is 40:25). As such, He maintains Himself at an inaccessible distance from His people, but He also possesses the power to create—after punishing—a magnificent newness (Is 55:5).

As a result of the communication of God's holiness, even things become holy. Everything pertaining to worship is holy: there are sacred times; the Temple, the Dwelling, and the Ark of the Covenant are holy: and there are sacred persons, such as priests, levites, etc.

In the New Testament holiness consists no longer in things or places but in the *manifestations of the Holy Spirit*. Jesus is called the "Holy One of God" (Lk 4:34). Before His birth He is called holy: "The One to be born of you [Mary] will be holy and called Son of the Most High" (Lk 1:35).

Holy means *belonging to God*, rendered legitimate or accredited by God. Hence, to resist Jesus is to resist God Himself. And Jesus, Son of God, "has out of boundless love become what we are so that we might become what He is" (St. Irenaeus).

To be a Saint means to receive as a gift something that forms part of God, something that God communicates to human beings in Jesus and through Jesus, giving them "the power to become children of God" (Jn 1:12). Holiness is something that overtakes human beings gratuitously and changes them substantially. The Bible describes this as a "new creation," "regeneration," "new life," "new birth," "adoption," and "eternal life."

### Saints in the Liturgy

The Church's view of sanctity can be seen in the celebrated passage of St. John Chrysostom cited by St. Augustine: "[The newly baptized] who a short time ago were prisoners now enjoy a sure freedom. Those who were lost wanderers are now citizens of the Church. Those who were mired in the confusion of sin are now entrenched in the well-being of justice. Indeed, they are not only free but also *saints*; not only saints but also just; not only just, but also children [of God]; not only children but also heirs; not only heirs but also members; not only members but also temples and organs of the Holy Spirit."[59]

For the Church sanctity is a gift which is accessible to all Christians; it is the normal state of human life elevated to a mysterious and stupendous supernatural dignity. It is the newness brought as a gift by Christ to all humankind, redeemed by Him in faith and grace (cf. Rm 6:4).

Sanctity is not only a gift but a duty as well. Presupposing that the Divine gift of grace makes us holy, sanctity becomes an obligation and the most binding experience of our freedom. "Christians must, with God's help, preserve, perfect, and live the sanctity they have received."[60]

Sanctity is far from passive. It is a positive impelling vocation because of the human beings' elevation to the level of children of God: "Be perfect as your heavenly Father is perfect," declares Jesus (Mt 5:48), and Paul adds, "as befits Saints" (Ep 5:3).

In time, the Church began to reserve the title "Saint" for one who died for Christ (4th century) and later for one who with good reason was believed to be with God after death. Since the 17th century, persons can be fully pronounced "Saints" only by the Pope and solely after a detailed scrutiny for signs of the heroic nature of their virtues. The Pope then declares in the Name of the Church that the Christians in question enjoy the vision of God in heaven and we can honor them as models and intercessors.

In keeping with this twofold concept, the Church began to celebrate Mass at the tombs of the Martyrs, keeping their birthdays into heaven, so to speak. She thus held up their virtues for the faithful to imitate and asked their intercession for the living.

Such memorials were inserted into the Paschal Mystery of Christ which is renowned over the course of the Liturgical Year. But they in no way break its unity or diminish its centrality. They place that mystery in a clearer light.

Every form of holiness proceeds from Christ and flows back to Him. All the Saints have in one way or another given their lives for Him. They have also exemplified one aspect of the infinite holiness of Christ.

Through such liturgical celebrations, the Church enables us to imitate the individual virtues of the Saints and to ask their intercession with Christ Who lives to make intercession for us with the Father.

In time the Church added other Saints besides martyrs to the feasts of Mary and the apostles. The Saints have put on Christ completely, "the great and invisible athlete," as the Christians of Lyons declared in 177 with respect to St. Blandina. To use the words of the early Christians of Smyrna: "We adore Christ because He is the Son of God; we love the Martyrs [Saints] because they are disciples and imitators of our Lord."

This has been the unchanging position of the Church toward the Saints, who embrace all states of life: ascetics, clergy, missionaries, laity. Each of them bears the image of God and reveals some Divine trait to us. Through each of them the Triune God deigned to reveal His image more fully to us in some respect.

Through a man, woman, or child who has surrendered fully to God's love, the unique Beauty shines forth in some way. If as St. Irenaeus says, "the glory of God consists in the life of a human being," no life more glorifies the Father, Son, and Holy Spirit than the life of a Saint.

The Saints are those members of Christ's Body who are the most closely united to Him. Each one has lived the words of St. Paul: "I live now yet it is no longer I but Christ who lives in me" (Gal 2:20). Each shows forth some aspect of Christ.

### Reform of Exaggerated Liturgical Cult of the Saints

During the last few pre-Vatican II centuries the liturgical cult of the saints had grown increasingly by leaps and bounds. As a result, it occupied a place in the Roman liturgy that was way out of proportion, actually supplanting feasts of our Lord which should hold the first place in our worship.

For example, the month of St. Joseph (March) supplanted the Season of Lent and the month of Mary (May) overshadowed the Season of Easter. In addition, there were 200 days on which the feast of the saints was obligatory—intruding on the theme of the Mystery of Christ being celebrated during the Seasons of the Year. In fact, until the initial reform of St. Pius X in 1913 the Feast of a Saint even displaced the Sunday celebration during the major seasons!

Little wonder that the Second Vatican Council strongly urged that the celebrations of the Saints be accorded their proper place in it rather than the disproportionate place they had come to possess.

Accordingly, the new Liturgical Calendar in the *Roman Missal* of Paul VI, issued in 1969 reduced the list of the Memorials or Feasts of Saints to modest proportions. There are now some 180 Saints honored universally with celebrations. Others are honored locally, as for example St. Frances Cabrini and St. Peter Claver in our country. In addition, the majority of such memorials are optional—they are left to the option of the priest and celebrating community to be chosen or not for celebration.

The General Instruction of the *Sacramentary (1974)* and that of the Liturgy of the Hours (1975) were also drawn up in such a way as to prevent the cult of the Saints in the future from ever again overshadowing the celebration of the Mysteries of the Lord.

Unfortunately, the action of the Conciliar and Post-conciliar Church in righting one wrong seems to have contributed to the birth of another. The saints were not only relegated to their proper place in the Liturgy; they lost that place too and sank into a kind of liturgical oblivion.

Some priest-celebrants have gone to the other extreme of ignoring the anniversaries of Saints even when they are obligatory Memorials in rank. This has also spawned a drive against images of the Saints in churches and chapels resulting in a "cold iconoclasm," to use the words of Pius XII.

For a time, such an attitude spilled over into the lives of ordinary Catholics, putting the Saints into the background. The prevailing opinion seemed to be that the Church had "devalued saints." After all, Philomena (a favorite saint of the Curé of Ars) was stricken from the ranks of the saints and Christopher among others was divested of his liturgical feast (but not his sainthood). Saints seemingly became dispensable, and devotion to them an embarrassment.

But this is not what the Church had said. And it is not what the Church says now. Her devotion to the Saints is as vital as ever, and we see signs that the devotion to the Saints is making a comeback among the people.

## The Saints—Our Models and Intercessors

The Saints hold a prominent place in the Liturgy of the Church. Every time we celebrate the Eucharist, we invoke their invisible presence: "Make us worthy to share eternal life/with Mary, the virgin mother of God,/with the apostles,/and with all the saints who have done your will throughout the ages./May we praise you in union with them,/and give you glory through your Son, Jesus Christ" (Eucharistic Prayer II).

The Saints are also our models and intercessors in the Liturgy. In the Preface for Holy Men and Women, the Church prays: "In their lives on earth/you give us an example./In our communion with them,/you give us their friendship./In their prayer for the Church/you give us strength and protection."

The Opening Prayers on the feasts of the Saints are particularly instructive in this regard. They recall the Saint's spirituality or summarize the Saint's mission in the Church and ask God to help His people through that Saint's intercession.

They thus enable us to imitate the virtues of the Saints just as they imitated Christ, for in their virtues there shines forth under different aspects the splendor of Jesus Christ. In a St. Thomas Aquinas we see the unparalleled wisdom of Christ; in a St. Thomas More, His marvelous humanity and good humor; in a St. Vincent de Paul, His overwhelming compassion. In a St. Teresa of Avila we glimpse the common sense of our Lord: in a St. Frances Cabrini, His zeal for souls; and in a St. Elizabeth Seton, His love for learning.

As Pius XII put it so well:

> The sacred Liturgy puts all these gems of sanctity before us so that we may consider them for our salvation, and rejoicing at their merits we may be inflamed by their example. It is necessary, then, to practice innocence in simplicity, concord in charity, modesty in humility, diligence in governing, readiness in helping those who

labor, mercy in serving the poor, constancy in defending truth, and justice in the strict maintenance of discipline, so that nothing may be wanting in us of the virtues that have been proposed for our imitation. These are the footprints left by the Saints in their journey homeward, so that guided by them we might follow them into glory.[61]

With the advent of the new *Roman Missal* the Church has put at our disposal another marvelous instrument for grasping the virtues of the Saints and imitating them in our lives. She has provided a more complete series of readings for the different categories of Saints.

It is the Word of God that points to the road taken by each Saint. It enables us to see it clearer and cling to it more tightly. At the same time, we are made to realize even more deeply how true it is that each Saint has something distinctive, some way of imitating Christ that is like no other!

## The Martyrs—Models of Christ the Martyr

The Christian faith is based on the startling affirmation of Jesus who died to save all human beings and *bore witness* to the definitive victory of love in His Resurrection. It is the affirmation of God manifesting His creative power in this self-sacrificing and conquering love.

Jesus is the first *martyr*, the first Witness, the guarantee that life will win out over sin and evil.

Christian martyrs are not simply those who give their lives for the faith. They are those who have entered fully into the mystery of love revealed to them by their Lord. They are not content simply to hope that after death their cause will triumph. They experience the living reality that life triumphs in their death, for they can share this love. They are caught up in the movement of love that comes from the Father and they discover their identity with their master, reliving the Paschal Mystery in their bodies.

Our human categories fail in the presence of the heroic love of the martyrs. Completely overwhelmed by the "folly" of the Cross, they fulfill themselves totally in the freedom of Jesus Christ. They no longer see glory and the cross as two realities but as two faces of the one movement of grace. They become living Gospels of love.

Through the Liturgy, the martyrs fill us with admiration and they instruct us in the overwhelming love with which Christ will grip us if we but grip Him. They show to what extent a life of faith can lead—to total selflessness and life in Christ (even without the bodily death).

The martyrs bear witness that the cries of the innocent are heard, that with God there are no "forgotten" deaths—even the deaths of the seemingly most lowly and most useless. In Jesus, the diminutions of history take on a meaning.

By martyrdom disciples are transformed into images of their Master by freely accepting death for the salvation of the world—as well as their conformity to Christ in the shedding of their blood. Though few are presented with such an opportunity, nevertheless all must be prepared to make this Profession of Faith even in the midst of persecution, which will never be lacking to the Church, in following the way of the Cross.[62]

### Pastors—In the Line of Christ the Good Shepherd

The pastors honored in the Liturgy are nothing more than a reflection of the Good Shepherd, the eternal High Priest and Guardian of our souls. The word pastor is kept because it has nuances that make it more appropriate than "leader" or "manager." It connotes a carrying out of a ministry in imitation of the unique Shepherd, Jesus Christ.

Thus, the pastors evangelized, taught, united, and built up the churches entrusted to them. We might say they were specialists in mass media for religion, experts in group dynamics, and first-class managers!

All this was guided not by secular concerns but by *pastoral* ones. Their words and activities were linked with and pointed to the Word of God and the sacraments. This is how they provided spiritual nourishment and help for the Church.

Yet despite all this their holiness stemmed ultimately from their obedience to the Lord and their docility to the Spirit Who achieves all holiness. They remain witnesses for us of the fundamental way of becoming holy—working with the Holy Spirit in our life situation.

Pastors are servants, in imitation of Christ Himself. They are our fathers and brothers in the Faith. They are also members of the flock of Christ. St. Peter's reaction to the cured sick man who prostrated Himself at Peter's feet was: "I am nothing but a man myself!" (Ac 10:26). Called out of the midst of God's people, they prompt all of us to discover our own mission in the *service of those around us*.

### Doctors—Imitators of Christ the Teacher

In a sense, all Christians are, by virtue of our Baptism, theologians—those who speak about or bear witness to God. We are all called to be

Saints, to say something about God in our own inimitable existence, in our own unique situation, and in our own proper way. St. Thomas Aquinas, one of the greatest of the doctors, was quick to say that a poor aged person who prayed could know more about the Faith than a professional theologian—and perhaps much more!

We can learn much from the doctors who were *ex professo* teachers of the faith, witnesses to Christ by their *communication skills* as well as by their lives. They were *Saints first, teachers second*, or they were teachers *through* being saints. Their knowledge and their genius would have been nothing without the love of God and human beings that was the source of all their genuine knowledge.

Yet the doctors' main contribution was the expertise in investigating and explicating the divine mystery in the ideas and words of their age. They thus contributed in an irreplaceable way to celebrating the *God of Wisdom and Truth*.

As experts in Scripture, theology, and the spiritual life, they received the questions of their brothers and sisters in search of light and gave correct responses. They accepted the challenge of setting out on a difficult adventure—the adventure of thought—and pursued it with courage amid snares of all kinds.

The feasts of doctors teach us to utilize our talents to proclaim Christ to others, to pursue the world for Christ, to find Him in every part of our lives—whether it be in *formal knowledge* or in *everyday living*. They inspire us to be doctors of the everyday love of God in our lives. This point is incisively made by the following incident. When St. Thomas Aquinas was asked by Christ in a vision what he desired as a reward for having written so brilliantly about Him, the Angelic Doctor replied: "You alone, O Lord!"

### Virgins—Imitators of Christ the Celibate

The Second Vatican Council set forth the underlying reason for the Church's veneration of virgins (and celibates):

> The holiness of the Church is fostered in a special way by the observance of the counsels proposed in the Gospel by our Lord to His disciples. An eminent position among these is held by virginity or the celibate state. This is a precious gift of Divine grace given by the Father to certain souls, whereby they may devote themselves the more easily to God alone, owing to an undivided heart.

This perfect continency, out of desire for the Kingdom of heaven, has always been held in particular honor in the Church. The reason for this was and is that perfect continency for the love of God is an incentive to charity, and is certainly a particular source of spiritual fecundity in the world.[63]

In creating the order of Virgins, the ancient Church responded to the paganism of the time with its priestesses and its vestal virgins. However, the Christian virginity was not a better copy of the pagan institutions.

By the gift of her whole life, the Christian virgin showed that she sought to prefer nothing to God's work and Christ's love. She participated in the folly of the Cross. She seemed to lose her life yet gained it and God's Kingdom in the process. She pointed to the wedding of the Eternal with the Human, which Jesus Himself had inaugurated.

Virgins as Saints bear witness to a love that surpasses all other loves. This love comes from God Himself and although it is expressed in human relations, is much more fundamental. Virgins call the world back to the first love—God—in all other loves, telling us that the only reason for love is the God of love!

The Liturgy thus reminds us that Virgins are irreplaceable in manifesting all the dimensions of God's love as it takes hold of human beings. They are, as it were, living parables inviting us to imitate those "wise" Virgins who await the coming of the Bridegroom—with faith and alert action (Mt 25:1-13).

## Men and Women Saints—Imitators of Christ's Humanity

On reaching this last category of Saints in the Liturgy, we might get the impression that we are leaving the world of the elite Saints and descending to the world of "lower level" Saints. The term "Men and Women Saints" seems to indicate that the Church had decided to lump together a group of Saints that she did not really know how to classify.

Nothing could be further from the truth. In actual fact, the liturgical texts chosen for the feasts of these Saints show to what extent *Sanctity* escapes all human labeling and pigeon-holing. God's call raises up men and women living in completely unique, ever new, and absolutely original situations. It is the reflection of God's infinite freedom.

This fact tells us graphically that each believer (who is, as we have seen, also called to be a Saint) has a proper vocation, a specialization in the faith and in life, that cannot be equated with that of any other believer. Each is a wonderful imitator of Christ's unique humanity.

Christ lived life to the full. He was truly the complete human being, the Man for others. He took advantage of every situation of life to bring people to God. In the words of Vatican II, "[Christ] animates, purifies, and strengthens the noble longings by which the human family strives to make its life more human and to render the whole earth submissive to this goal."[64]

It is God's plan that the Church should "contribute greatly toward making the family of human beings and its history more human."[65] In the final analysis, whoever "follows after Christ, the perfect Man, becomes more of a human being."[66]

These saints show us vividly how all the human can be transformed in Christ. They used the world *totally*—yet they used it for God, as a world that is "passing away" (1 Cor 7:31), one that looks forward to completion in the next life, in eternity.

Like all the Saints, the holy people in this category are hearers and doers of the divine Word. It is that Word that called them. It is that Word that inspired their unique vocation in them. That same Word led them to discover in the very circumstances of their lives the right way for them to respond to God's love. In honoring them in the Liturgy, we ask the same thing for ourselves!

Chapter 15
# THE SACRAMENTS AND SACRAMENTALS: CHRISTIFYING THE UNIVERSE

For Christians, Christ's coming and mission have a consecratory character and purpose. Christ has given us a sacramental world, and Christians are to grow into the perfection of Christ by means of sacramental action.

In a sacramental action, nature and grace combine to elevate and transform the creatures of God. This is the Liturgy, in which God is worshiped and glorified, and human beings are made partakers of the light and Kingdom of God.

In every sacramental act there is a hierarchy of being among the various elements that unites them in an efficacious religious act. The first element is Jesus Christ, Who vivifies and leavens the other elements of the act through the Holy Spirit. The second is human beings who are equipped with wonderful powers of reason, sentiment, and emotions as well as capabilities of sense, hearing, voice, singing and speaking, motion and gestures. The third is inanimate creation—bread, wine, water, oil, light, incense, vestments, gold, bells and organ.

All these elements unite to give glory to the Blessed Trinity—praise to the Father, through the Son, in the Holy Spirit. At the same time, this act accomplishes the sanctification intended, signified, and accomplished by the sacramental rite.

This sacramental system includes both the seven sacraments and the sacramentals. The sacraments can in one way or another be traced back to Christ. So can some of the sacramentals—for example, the *washing of the feet* on Holy Thursday.

Another way of looking at this point is to say that the seven sacraments owe their institution to the personal historical Christ whereas the sacramentals owe it to the mystical Christ—Jesus living and working in His mystical body, the Church. Thus, sacramentals are extensions and radiations of the sacraments.

Both are sources of divine life. Both have the same purpose—divine life. Both have the identical cause—the death and resurrection of Christ. But they differ from one another in nature, efficacy, and intensity.

In the nature of things, Christians can make use of sacramentals to continue the work of the sacraments or prepare for their reception. This is especially true of new blessings that will be forthcoming when the new rite of blessings (that is part of the *Roman Ritual*) is published. In accord with the specific mandate of the Second Vatican Council, it should have blessings that lay people can perform and that have a direct link to their daily lives.

The sprinkling of holy water at the beginning of the Sunday Eucharist and the blessing of infants and children are prolongations of the sacrament of baptism. And Benediction of the Blessed Sacrament is a prolongation of the Eucharist. Blessings of a school, a library, or a typewriter are extensions of the sacrament of Confirmation, and the Consecration of Virgins is a follow-up of the sacrament of Holy Orders.

The Confiteor at Mass, the papal blessing at the hour of death, and exorcisms are prolongations of the sacrament of Penance. And the blessing of the sick as well as the blessing of oil, medicine, and linens are extensions of the sacrament of the Anointing of the Sick.

Finally, the blessings of a bridal-chamber, of an expectant mother, and of various materials in a home are prolongations of the sacrament of Matrimony.

Neither the sacraments nor the sacramentals are magic formulas. Their effect in one way or another depends on us. Only if we use them with true faith and genuine devotion will they really achieve the purpose for which Christ has left them to us and the Church has authorized their use.

### Christ, the Sacrament of the Encounter with God

Every encounter of human beings with God (except the one in the mysterious and ineffable communion in the innermost depths of persons) takes place in the events of a human individual or a people, and in the symbolic actions which constitute a remembrance of that event.

Every communication, every contact between human beings takes place through gestures, words, and actions. We can only open up to others in order to encounter them by using concrete things or actions. But these are ambiguous for the most part. This is the reason for words. They explain the actions performed and help people understand the depth of the gesture made.

God has communicated Himself to us through gestures, actions, and words which we call sacraments. They are gestures of God through the Spirit. God's great sacramental gesture was to become man. Hence, Christ is the first and the true sacrament, because He is the efficacious sign of the divinization of humankind.

In the Incarnation, in Jesus of Nazareth, a human nature is elevated to the divine dignity. This took place not for Jesus alone—for He is the Word of God from eternity and for all eternity—but for us as well.

Christ is the sign, the type, the model of the divine filiation to which God wants to elevate all human beings.

He is the efficacious sign because He comes "to gather together all the dispersed children of God" (Jn 11:25), to unite them with Him in a single Body, the Body of Christ. He thus becomes "the eldest of a multitude of brothers and sisters" (Rm 8:29) whom He enables by his death-resurrection to share in all that he has and all that he is.

It is absolutely true that Christ is God and all that he did as man is an act of the Son of God, and an act of God. However, we must not imagine that Christ's divinity shone visibly through His body. Without faith His contemporaries saw Him only as a man.

In order for them to encounter Jesus as God-Man, they needed faith. They needed the eyes of faith and a heart open to God, capable of reading His human actions as *signs of God*.

The followers of Jesus did not see God all at once in our Lord's words and His behavior. Only gradually was the mystery of His person made known to them—the mystery of God's presence and compassion.

This is what Jesus indicated in His reply to Philip who asked Him to show the Father to His disciples: "How long I have been with you, Philip, and you still do not know Me. He who sees Me sees the Father also" (Jn 14:8f).

Slowly the disciples, and then the Church, came to realize that the love of the Man Jesus is in effect the human incarnation of God's redeeming love, a coming of God's love in visible form. Thus, because the human actions of Jesus are actions of God, they possess a divine power of salvation. They are salvific, causes of grace.

And since this divine form appears to human beings under an earthly and visible form, the saving actions of Jesus are *sacramental*. For sacrament signifies a divine gift of salvation and through a very palpable form, which concretizes the gift.

All the actions of Jesus during His earthly life are ultimately intended to give life—eternal life. This is the message of the Resurrection that He worked: "I am the Resurrection and the Life" (Jn 11:25).

These actions will perdure until the end of the world. For Christ, the sacrament of our encounter with God, is still with us to work those saving actions for us through the sacraments of the Church.

### The Church—Sacrament of the Encounter with Christ

The Church is the continuation of the "Israel of old"—she is the new People of God, "a chosen race, a royal priesthood, a holy nation" (1 P 2:9). As such, she is born of the Holy Spirit through faith and the sacraments.

She is herself the sacrament of Jesus Christ, just as Christ is the Sacrament of our encounter with God. Risen and ascended into heaven, Jesus continues to be active in the world and to communicate with all human beings through the Church:

> Rising from the dead, [Christ] sent His life-giving Spirit upon His disciples and through Him has established His Body which is the Church as the *universal* Sacrament of salvation. Sitting at the right hand of the Father, He is continually active in the world so that He may lead human beings to the Church, and through her join them to Himself and so that He may make them partakers of His glorious life by nourishing them with His own Body and Blood.[67]

Twentieth century theologians (and Vatican II as well) have given the word sacrament a wider meaning, one that is more supple and more traditional, embracing all the realities of the history of the world, in which the mystery of salvation is revealed because it is lived.

Thus, the Church is in Christ like a Sacrament or like a sign and instrument both of a very closely knit union with God and of the unity of the human race.[68]

The Church and Christ form one single body while remaining two separate entities. The Church is a reminder of Christ just as a spouse is a reminder of her husband. She is not Christ but a sign and sacrament of Christ. She proclaims Christ and it is in her that Christ is encountered.

## The Sacraments and Sacramentals: Christifying the Universe 135

This union with Christ and through Him with God is the Kingdom of God. The Church recognizes the Kingdom already present in the world. She embraces it in joy and thanksgiving. She labors to extend it to all people, and does this through the sacraments.

The sacraments rightly celebrated bring the hope of the Church to the world. They are advance signs of the success and completion of the world in Jesus Christ. Thus, just as the Incarnate Christ was the visage of the Father, so the Church is the visage of the risen and ascended Christ for all people on earth. She is the efficacious sign, the sacrament, that renders Him present to the world.

This is what she accomplishes in her sacraments and it is this mystery that she calls us to live: to be a sign of a *Love* that surpasses us.

### Operative Signs or Indicators

Liturgical rites may be regarded as above all *actions or gestures*. They are certainly not mere spectacles. Their primary role is not to communicate something to someone who is there as a spectator. They are of the order of *praxis*—but a praxis that presupposes and contains a communication without which they would lose their identity.

This communication is made possible in two different ways. The first is through the Liturgy of the Word that has now been included and amplified in every sacramental rite. This is the phenomenon of communication in an assembled group and necessitates a distinction of roles.

Within the community the structure "teacher and taught" is ultimately a symbol of God who speaks to His people. The community does not speak to itself; it listens. The Bible and the Church's teaching office (Magisterium) that authenticates it have a role in the assembly, because the book and the office are both founded on the community's faith. Hence, there is a circuit of communication within the community, thanks to a diversification of roles.

The Liturgical Action flows from this distinction of roles and the circuit of communication. It is not a spontaneous demonstration of a crowd—it is a social institution. Thus, these circuits of communication are at the service of the Liturgical action.

This highlights the second way in which the communication of the rites is made possible. Each Liturgical Action itself communicates. Each has a denotation and a connotation. It is a praxis which becomes *significative*. It expresses one thing and points to another through it. The Eucharist, for example, is a true community meal, even when this meal is highly stylized. But at the same time it connotes communion with Christ and with others, through participation in the Paschal Mystery.

The Liturgical Rite is not merely an action that refers only to the present. Neither is it an action that has a vague reference to a time past. It is an action that has a definite relation with an historical existence, Jesus Christ, and with an event, the Paschal Mystery of His Death and Resurrection. In the Liturgical Action, this historical event is lived in a mysterious way.

The Liturgical Action is an *indicator* of a historical referent. Signs represent; they do not, strictly speaking, *indicate*. Indicators, however, do re-present something. They do not do this like a billboard along a highway but like some element that is really related, in one way or another, to the reality which it recalls.

A billboard with the figure of a man taking pictures is a sign. It represents a man and a camera. But a footprint in the sand is an *indicator*. It tells us there was someone there. Starting with the elements furnished by the imprint, we can unearth a certain amount of information—not about man in general—but about the *particular person* who left this imprint. Between a signifier and the signified there can only be a *relation of reason*. But between an indicator and the thing indicated there is always a *relation that is real*.

In the Liturgical Rites, the elements which indicate their relation to Jesus Christ and His Paschal Mystery do not function as mere signs or symbols even though those are the usual words used to describe them. They really function as *indicators* in the technical sense described above. In most cases they function as both signs *and* indicators.

Thus, in the Eucharist, the community meal in memory of Christ is not only a sign of the communion of all in Christ. It is also an *indicator* because the elements used for the meal are the very ones that Christ used, as if in response to Christ's mandate: "Do this in memory of Me." And through the power of Christ's Spirit, they place us in touch with the reality they indicate.

### Signs of Faith

The sacraments are efficacious signs of the Covenant of God with human beings, that is, they both reveal and realize it at the same time. In the celebration of the sacraments, the risen Jesus is really present. Through actions and words which "signify" His presence and His actions,

## The Sacraments and Sacramentals: Christifying the Universe 137

He communicates to us the intention of salvation that He pursues in the world, and that he is in the process of achieving in us here and now.

He also indicates the dispositions and life attitude that He expects from us in the Covenant event that He proposes to us in each sacrament. He helps us *with power*. This is the sacramental grace that flows from each sacrament.

None of this is visible; it must be inferred; it depends on faith. First the faith of the Church. Without the faith of the Church, there is no sacrament. This is what is known as the intention of the minister *to do what the Church wants* in any sacrament—which is in turn what Christ wants.

Such faith is what makes the sacraments efficacious by themselves (*ex opere operato*), by the very power of their positing. So long as this faith is present, the sacraments are really acts of Christ who comes to encounter us. Nothing is lacking from His part. The Liturgy is a dialogue; it cannot be one-sided. Another faith is needed to make the sacraments fulfill their effect *in people*—the faith of the recipients.

Without the faith of the adult recipient of a sacrament, there is no efficacious encounter with Christ, no reception of sacramental grace. Without faith the recipient, as it were, spurns God's invitation.

The sole exception is infant Baptism where the faith is presumed and expressed by the adults present—the parents, godparents, or the administrator of the sacrament. The reason is that Baptism gives a sacramental *character* that can be activated, so to speak, when the child reaches the use of reason and can consent to the reception of Baptism and the encounter with Christ.

Two other sacraments have such a character—Confirmation and Holy Orders. These can be received without having the necessary dispositions—faith and state of grace. They can be revived at some future occasion when the dispositions become present.

In their case, there is an intermediate effect in addition to the greatest effect of the sacrament that is grace, and which depends on the consent of the individual who alone is sanctified by it. The intermediate effect is a *character* which is not ordered toward the good of the recipient but to the worship and organization which the individual shares with others. Therefore, the sacramental character is *permanent* and *independent* of the personal dispositions of the recipient.

However, without faith the sacraments are useless *to those who receive them*. And this faith is essentially faith in Christ the Redeemer—an explicit faith in Jesus Christ who died and rose for the salvation of all human beings.

In the final analysis, the sacraments must be celebrated *in spirit and in truth*. *In spirit* means not a disembodied worship but a worship whose ceremonies have a meaning, inspire devotion, suggest the mystery of God, elevate the soul, and give it a sense of consecration.

*In truth* means a true preaching of the Gospel through the sacraments, one in which the external expressions are regulated logically and in a way that imparts the real meaning of the rite to the people.

### Personal Encounters with Christ

In every sacrament, the Jesus who touches us—who pardons, heals, invests us with His priesthood, or with His love—is always the Jesus of the Paschal Mystery, the Jesus eternally established in what is the culminating part of His life and His right to glory—the event of His Death and Resurrection. Every sacrament plunges us *spiritually but really* into the very act of Jesus dying to sin and rising to new life. Hence, each sacrament—not only the Eucharist—is a Memorial of the Death and Resurrection of Jesus Christ.

As we have seen, Jesus is really present to us today. The sacraments make Him *personally present* to the recipient. Faith makes this presence live for us through the sacraments. We meet Jesus, we become transformed in Him, and we become conformed to Him in the manner proper to each sacrament.

Accordingly, we must prepare to encounter Him corporally but symbolically with faith and love:

1) in the Scripture proclaimed and the Word announced: "He who hears you hears Me" (Lk 10:16);

2) in the sole fact of gathering together in His Church to celebrate Him: "Where two or three are gathered together in My Name, there am I in their midst" (Mt 18:20);

3) in the Sacrament of Baptism: "Go teach all nations, baptizing them in the Name of the Father, and of the Son, and of the Holy Spirit" (Mt 28:16);

4) in the sacrament of the Eucharist: "Take and eat. . . . Take and drink. . . . Do this in Memory of Me" (Mt 26:26; Lk 22:19);

5) in the fraternal correction and reconciliation in the community: "Whatever you loose on earth shall be loosed in heaven" (Mt 18:18);

"Receive the Holy Spirit: whose sins you shall forgive they are forgiven" (Jn 20:22-23);
6) and in the other sacraments.

Only the eyes of faith can discern the true Presence of Jesus in this world. The Lord awaits us but our human eyes are prevented from seeing Him. It takes our entire person to encounter Christ in this world. The sacraments are our indicators to Christ. They facilitate our encounter with Him.

We must listen with openness to His Word and participate wholeheartedly in the sacramental Action. Through that Word and that action, the Lord himself draws near to us, speaks to us, and becomes united with us. We must be willing to meet Christ on His terms, not ours. For it is not we who go out to meet Christ but He who comes to meet us.

In this encounter, we must be ready to be transformed. When God meets human beings, they are inevitably changed for the better. They put on a new life. In order to encounter Christ we must accept the law of the Paschal Mystery in our life—the law of life through death.

Each sacrament plunges the Paschal Mystery in the realities of our individual lives. It thus demands that we be freely disposed to embrace the *conversion* that alone gives new life. We must seek God more than self: "He who seeks only himself brings himself to ruin [loses his life]. But he who brings himself to nought [loses his life] for Me discovers who he is" (Mt 10:39).

The practical sign of this acceptance is that our encounter with Christ in any sacrament goes on to bear fruit in our earthly lives—that it makes us better witnesses for Christ to our human brothers and sisters, that they too can run to meet Christ along their pilgrim journey.

## "Celebration" of the Sacraments

The sacraments are sacred actions comprised of *word and expression* and they are to be made part of our lives. They are to be expressed in Liturgy and lived in life. This means that we do not have a simple "administration" of each sacrament—but a "celebration."

Such a view is an apt reminder that faith is a gift, something that comes to encounter us from God, and the sacraments are *freely given* us by God. Hence, like all Liturgical celebrations, the sacraments have a festive character about them, a character of gratuity, and "non-utility," a character of contemplation and "play" about them.

We live in the most technologically oriented age. People are trying desperately to avoid being enslaved by what is useful, technological, and consumerish. They fervently cry out: "Celebrate life." This means to realize that there is more to life than production, work, and technological progress.

Life is in the final analysis a gift to be grasped and explored and appreciated. Life is permeated with spirit, with joy, with love, and with mystery.

The Liturgy points out that gratuitousness in life comes from God in Jesus and the Spirit. It is ultimately the very life of God, His love, His freedom, and His Kingdom. The Liturgy tells us to seek God first (that is, life's gratuities) and all life's necessities will come in due time—they will fall in their rightful place. This reminder inspires on our part a feeling of praise and thanks.

The Liturgy is not disconnected from daily life. It also reminds us that the other "non-gratuitous" part of our lives is still needed. It remains anchored in the History of Salvation.

What we celebrate is neither the life nor the love that always exists but the *action* of a particular person, Jesus (that is, the Life, Death, and Resurrection). It took place at a definite time in history and is now made present for us.

The sacramental celebration incorporates real historical actions that are outside the subject of the action. In them there is pursued, actualized, and manifested the historical action of Jesus that comprised His Redemption.

Celebration is always a communal one. It is the celebration of the Church through the particular community in which the sacrament is being celebrated. Every sacrament is given and received under the aegis of the local community in which the celebrants are members.

Thus every sacrament increases the faith of the community, deepens its piety, and helps to break down the barriers that divide faceless congregations. It builds up their common bonds in faith and love and manifests the Church at work in the world.

## The Efficacious Word

The single point common to the celebration of all the sacraments is that each has a "form"—a formula that expresses its meaning. Some sacramental rites use *material elements*: water, bread and wine, oil. Others use a

## The Sacraments and Sacramentals: Christifying the Universe

*gesture*: Sign of the Cross, imposition of hands. Still others, like marriage, require *neither elements nor particular gestures*. However, all require the *word*, to state what God is accomplishing in each sacrament.

Hence, to confect a sacrament the word is primary. It is the *word* or form—the word of faith that we preach—that makes the sacraments sacred, capable of dispensing grace.

This word of the sacraments, however, is the Word of God. It is the Word of God who is present, who challenges, calls, commits Himself, and transforms us and, as we have seen, every Word of God is an act of God.

This Word is all the more efficacious since it is a Person: the Son. In the sacraments, therefore, the Word is not limited to expressing the meaning of the signs nor even to accomplishing them. Since it is the Word, it is the *very meaning* of the sacrament.

Thus, the important thing is not to exhaust ourselves in seeking a holy priest to celebrate with. For Christ is always there personally in each sacrament, and He is the all-Holy. Neither should we run from Mass to Mass, from absolution to absolution, as if the sacraments had been devalued.

The important thing is to let ourselves be "worked on" by the sacrament: to get our faith into it, to really thirst for it, to listen to it, to enter into it with the best possible dispositions—and then to *wait*—to let the sacrament flow over into our lives.

To be a Christian is not to be less a human being. God became human to encounter us in human relationships, that is, relationships that are expressed in rites, symbols, and feasts. As such, there is a *particular* sacrament.

The moment is the very moment of the celebration. But this sacrament must open up to a *time that perdures*. At the moment of celebration, everything is placed as if in a germ or a seed but it must be lived out in a whole lifetime.

> Just as the rain and the snow
>     come down from the heavens
> And do not return there
>     until they have watered the earth
>     and made it fertile and fruitful,
> Giving seed to those who sow
>     and bread to those who eat,
> So shall it be with My Word
>     that goes forth from My mouth.

It shall not return to me empty,
    but shall do My will,
    and achieve the goal for which I sent it.

(Is 55:10-11)

Chapter 16
# THE LITURGY OF THE HOURS: THE SANCTIFICATION OF TIME

A fact that very few Catholics advert to is that there is only one "Sacrifice (or Prayer) of Praise" and it has diverse expressions. The Mass is the culmination and source of every prayer of praise, and the Liturgy of the Hours (Divine Office) is the complement of the Eucharist.

This organic unity must be reflected in the manner in which the Mass and Office are celebrated. The priest, for example, is no longer only a celebrant of the sacrifice who completes and concentrates in a definite time of day his essential ministry to "form" the community around the table that unites believers in a single body. He is also the person who continually offers thanksgiving and gratitude to God for his people, in every hour of the day, or at least at the most significant phases of the daily rhythm: morning, midday, evening, and night.

Thus, the Liturgy of the Hours must be oriented toward the Eucharist, since it enkindles and fosters those attitudes that are necessary for a beneficial Eucharistic Celebration: a spirit of faith, hope, love, devotion, and sacrifice.[69] Above all, the Divine Office is the prolongation of the Eucharistic Mystery spread out over the major hours of the day.[70]

The Liturgy of the Hours is a prayer that is pastorally tailored in a most varied way to the communitary needs of the prayer of the people. Above all, it enables the people to see that the Eucharistic Celebration cannot be exhausted in the ample time of the communitary celebrations, but must be extended and diffused to all the times of the day.

The Eucharistic Prayer—in its etymological meaning of thanksgiving—must pervade and dominate all other forms of prayer insofar as it imprints on them a tone and a preeminence of the awe-inspiring gratuitousness of God's wondrous deeds remembered and recapitulated in the Paschal Memorial.

However, this is possible only through the Liturgy of the Hours, which itself has praise as its paramount theme, ever comprising all the possible meanings of prayer that human beings can experience in the praise of God: reverence, adoration, trust, joy, gratitude, petition, and compunction.

This intrinsic relationship between the Eucharistic Liturgy and the Liturgy of the Hours in the most communitary sense is beautifully expressed by the insertion of the Our Father "at the end of the Intercessions in the two chief Hours, Morning Prayer and Evening Prayer."[71] It is the most solemn and most authoritative prayer of the Christian Faith, which sums up the whole Gospel and which liturgical tradition has always regarded as the immediate preparation for the Sacramental consummation of the Eucharistic Sacrifice.

### A Liturgy "of the Hours"

This Liturgy that complements the Eucharist has various names (Work of God, Divine Office, and Sacrifice of Praise among others), but its most suitable name is "Liturgy of the Hours." It deals with "Hours," that is, temporal articulations of the day. Each part of this Liturgy has for its purpose to sanctify a particular moment or part of the day. And this is not some secondary or peripheral aspect. It is an essential one that is important for our spiritual lives.

Time has both a cosmic dimension and a human and existential one. It is the indispensable reality within which our life unfolds.

Time provides the framework in which things happen. It gives our lives their historical dimension, their *here and now* character.

The Liturgy of the Hours accompanies the day with a rhythm of prayer by choosing characteristic moments of daily life. It gives the Divine an opportunity to make its way into the very texture of our days.

Following the Gospel ideal based on Christ's words to "pray always" (Lk 18:1), the Church seeks to embrace time in its entirety by linking prayer with the basic temporal articulations of the day as effected by the circling of the planets and the rhythm of human life.

The Liturgical Year, which informs both the Liturgy of the Mass and the Liturgy of the Hours is, from the historical and the theological standpoint, very distinct from the sanctification of time effected by the Liturgy of the Hours. In the cyclical course of yearly feasts—to which the Biblical readings especially refer—the "Sacrament of Salvation" produces a spiritual joy or exultation in the Faith which generates in us a special contact with the mysteries of Christ. Formally, it is a question of almost a doctrinal communication through which the doctrine of the mystery of Christ is intimately connected with the memorial of the consecrated day.

The sacramentality of the Divine Office, which selects a few hours of the quasi-material fabric of the entire day in order to sanctify them by attributing a specific significance to such *hours*, assumes as a material element the light of day that becomes the visible sign of the two aspects of the Memorial of Christ.

Christ is first the light of the divine knowledge infused into us, the Author and Finisher of our faith (Heb 12:2). He is also the light in which the glory of God communicated to us through His Resurrection shines forth.

Thus the *hour* marked by prayer is transported out of the empty flow of cosmic time into the sphere of the divine, and those who experience such an *hour* acquire roots in eternity. At the same time, the *hour* in question applies its specific significance and natural charm to the prayer.

At *dawn*, the world is, as it were, *created anew*, after a night of darkness and inactivity. We too are filled with new spiritual energy. We pray that the light may shine in our hearts, as we experience a resurrection and renewed confidence.

*Midday* has the connotation of heat and light (the "noonday sun"), inevitably recalling God, the Light beyond all shadows. We see this light as the symbol of the Spirit and truth and grace, which throw a spiritual radiance about the universe.

*Evening* brings darkness and rest from labor. It reminds us that God knows no rest from His work ("My Father is at work till now"—Jn 5:17). Even in darkness, He continues to watch lovingly over us (Ps 64:8).

This night is lit up like the day, because Christ the "eternal Day" is ever with us. The alternation of light and darkness reminds us of the inconstancy of all that is human. But it also helps ground us on God.

Such themes are completely alien to many of us. For the pace and character of modern life have replaced human adaptation to the rhythms of the universe and the material world.

By utilizing the Liturgy of the Hours we can begin anew to appreciate these "traces" of God in natural creation. Indeed, we will enable creation to sing God's praises with us together with the angels and the Saints—for we are to offer praise "in the name of every creature under heaven" (Eucharistic Prayer IV).

## Salvation History Bound Up with Time

The "Hours" are also bound up with the Mystery of Christ. This mystery binds the whole History of Salvation into a unity. It is at the center of human history and is connected with the rhythms of the year.

It is actualized in the celebration of the Liturgical Year and the moments of the day through the Hours:

> These hours (*horae*) are laid down according to the sun's course; as we have said, the sun is a symbol of Christ. Historical occurrences from the life of Jesus yield symbolic meaning, or fall in with such meanings. Thus the sun's rising is the most striking image of the Savior rising from the dead, and in fact the hour of His rising; Sext, the time he was nailed to the cross, but according to ancient tradition the hour of his ascension as well, the high noon of his life; None was the hour at which he died on the cross. At the third hour of the day, Terce recalls the outpouring of the Holy Spirit.[72]

Thus, the whole day becomes an ongoing celebration of the Mystery of Christ and is sanctified. The Liturgy of the Hours provides us with a convenient way for reliving all the stages of that Mystery.

However, it will only do so in reality if Christ is the habitual center of our life. And it must be a Christ who is not merely an historical person but also a person *living and present to us right now*. Through the Liturgy of the Hours the Church actualizes in herself and in us Christ's work of Redemption: "In the Holy Spirit, Christ carries out through the Church the work of human redemption and God's perfect glorification."[73]

Accordingly, every moment of our lives is a veritable "time of salvation" for us and for the whole Church—if we but take hold of it and use it.

## Prayer of Christ

In the words of Vatican II: "Christ Jesus, the High Priest of the new and eternal Covenant, took our human nature and introduced into the world of our exile that hymn of praise which is sung in the heavenly places throughout all ages."[74]

From that time on, the praise of God wells up from the heart of Christ in human words of adoration, propitiation, and intercession. He presents them to the Father as the head of a new humanity, mediator between God and humankind, in the name of all and for the good of all.

# The Liturgy of the Hours: The Sanctification of Time

As is evident from even a cursory look at the Gospels, Jesus' whole life was lived in communion with God. He went naturally from prayer to work and from work to prayer without ever losing that communion.

Now, seated at the right hand of the Father, He continues to pray for us. He intercedes for us (Rm 8:34), appears before God on our behalf (Heb 9:24), and is our advocate with the Father (1 Jn 2:1).

The Liturgy of the Hours is a continuation of Christ's prayer. It is the continuation in the Church of the eternal hymn of the Word, a hymn Christ brought with Him to earth. It is continued by the priesthood of the body of the Church in union with the head. Through Baptism and the anointing of the Holy Spirit, the baptized are consecrated as a spiritual temple and a holy priesthood, and they become able to offer the worship of the New Covenant.

In praying the Liturgy of the Hours our prayer and Christ's fuse into a single sigh to the Father. St. Augustine has put it in a beautiful way:

> When we speak to God in prayer we do not separate the Son from God, and when the Body of the Son prays it does not separate its Head from itself. It is the one Savior of His Body, our Lord Jesus Christ, the Son of God, Who Himself prays for us, and prays in us, and is the object of our prayer. He prays for us as our priest. He prays in us as our Head. And He is the Object of our prayer as our God. Let us then hear our voice in His voice, and His voice in ours.[75]

Thus, a lively participation in the Liturgy of the Hours should impart to us a desire to live out our identification with Christ in prayer, to feel that His prayer is being uttered through our mouth, just as His life resides in the life of grace in us. Inevitably, this will build up the unity between Christ and us and lead to a deeper spiritual life.

## Prayer of the Church

The Liturgy of the Hours is also a prayer of the Church, since Christ and Church are inseparable as Head and members. But this prayer is not a prayer of the Church *legally speaking* because it is endorsed by the official Church. It is a prayer of the Church because it is the Church community that *prays*.

Each of us is part of that "subject who prays" by the fact that we are members of the Church. This gives us the right and duty to express the prayer dimension as well as the kerygmatic, apostolic, and caritative dimensions of the Mystical Body.[76]

We pray this prayer as a community, never in isolation. The Liturgy of the Hours is always a community prayer and should lead to *communion* among those praying it. In this sense, it shapes the Church community.

This is an ideal, of course, and it is never perfectly reached. But even striving for it will insure that we will forget self in shared prayer. We will truly pray in tune with the Church.

We become interpreters of all her needs. In our tears, the Church weeps for all who mourn; in our joys, she rejoices with all who are glad; in our repentance, she does penance for all who repent. The main concerns of the Kingdom of God become our concerns. And the deepest cries of our beings are joined to the huge cry that springs forth from the believing, loving, exulting, sorrowing and hoping human race.

The Liturgy of the Hours is made up of many elements, and it is impossible to describe all of them at length. A few words about the outstanding ones, however, may be of benefit here.

### The Psalms

The major role is held by the Psalms. This alone would give the Liturgy of the Hours a unique hue, for the Psalms are the prayer of God's assembly, the public prayer par excellence of the People of God.

They can be regarded as the "Prayerbook of the Holy Spirit" Who inspired the psalmists to compose magnificent prayers and hymns for almost every religious desire and need, mood and feeling. In the words of St. Athanasius, "they have a unique value; most Scripture speaks *to* us whereas the Psalms speak *for* us."

The Psalms are Christ's prayer also. As a fervent Jew, He prayed them many times in the Liturgy of the Temple. At the same time, they also look to Christ—they are Christological. This feature is highlighted by the titles, the citations from the Fathers, the Antiphons, and the Glory Be, as well as by the Psalm-Prayers.

The Psalms provide the ascending aspect of the "Liturgy of Praise" together with the *Intercessions* of the major Hours which recommend to God the whole day at its beginning and intercede for the needs of the human and ecclesial community at its end.

### The Readings

The new Liturgy of the Hours better harmonizes the *ascending* aspect with a *descending* aspect of the "lectio divina," that is, with the place reserved for *meditative reading of the Word of God*. This ample part of the Office of Readings contributes in a decisive manner emphasizing the dialogal aspect of ecclesial prayer.

This reading is not so much a proclamation to move us to worship as it is a *lectio divina*, a reading and meditating of the Word of God. The Readings are primarily didactic. They are meant to be listened to in a spirit of openness and to shape our thinking as the Spirit wills.

In a sense, this reading has the character of a retreat or a day of recollection with the Holy Spirit as our guide. God still speaks to us *today*. There is a kind of inspiration in this reading (in accordance with an important stream of patristic thought) that looks upon it as an ever-present reality.

God's Word is now filled with the Spirit, whose influence is exercised no longer through the sacred writer but through the Word that is placed in my hands or sounded in my ears. However, this is only true *if we read* "in tune with the Church," which is the living organism that transmits the Word to us and is alone able, as if by some "instinct for the Divine," to grasp its full meaning.

We cannot approach this Word as mere spectators. We are not encountering a "piece of paper" or a "dead letter." We are attaining a personal encounter with the living God who addresses us and wants us to respond to Him.

This reading is a *dialogal, meditational, and prayerful* reading. At the same time, it is a reading that imparts wisdom—one that goes beyond mere scientific knowledge and wisdom. Finally, it is a reading that leads to *action*.

The Office includes not only scriptural and patristic readings but hagiographical readings as well. The Saints are "sacred pages" through which God addresses the world. They are "Gospels" endowed with a new realism because they are filled inwardly with the Spirit of Christ! The Saints are living interpretations of Scripture, bits of authentically existential exegesis.

### Responsories

In the Liturgy of the Hours the Scripture Reading carried out in a liturgical context receives its authentic interpretation guaranteed by the fact that it is ecclesial, thus eliminating the risk of subjective interpretation. But it also receives its fuller sacramental actuation.

Through the aid of feasts and memorials, the Word of God "celebrated" (accompanied by Psalms and Responsories, etc.)[77] is no longer solely God's revelation. It is also an *initiation* into the Mystery lived in the liturgical *today* of the Church.[78]

This means teaching those who pray the Liturgy of the Hours to meditate on the facts of Biblical and human history in accordance with the spirit that effects this passage from the historico-doctrinal (literal sense) to the "gnosis" or more substantial meditation of Scripture.[79] In this way, they will arrive at the spiritual sense and acquire the interior dispositions to relive it today by means of a personal response.

The new type of Responsory, therefore, has one of the following purposes: (1) It sheds light on the understanding of the reading that precedes it. (2) It situates that reading in Salvation History. (3) It projects on that reading the content of the Old and the New Testaments. (4) It turns the reading into prayer and contemplation.[80]

## The Hours and Daily Life

There are two ways of looking at the Office. One is that the structure of the Office determines the rhythm of work. The other is that the rhythm of life determines the times for common prayer.

This amounts to saying that we need both prayer and work. Hence, the best solution is the one that allows both truths the fullest possible recognition and harmonization.

In the new Office this harmonization is made easier. Morning Prayer, Daytime, Prayer, and Evening Prayer can readily be celebrated at their rightful times because they occur at points in the day that naturally call for a prayer and union with God.

The new Office includes options that help make it authentic. It helps our prayer well up in our hearts and at the same time arises from our concrete situations and daily lives. It insures continuity in our lives.

The Office allows for a word about the text of the Liturgy of the Hours and our real-life situation in the community, a homily that applies the Liturgy to life, intercessory prayers that are life-oriented, and optional psalms and readings that are more apropos in terms of the world situation, Church problems, or the special circumstances of the community.

Yet even with all these legitimate applications to life, the Liturgy is an encounter with Someone *outside our lives*. Although God comes to us in life, He stands outside it and calls us to surmount it. And the Liturgy of the Hours is first and foremost the praise of God.

### Action and Prayer

Jesus has given us the example of a life balanced perfectly on action and prayer. "Each day's work was closely connected with His prayer and in fact flowed out of that prayer.... The Divine Master showed that prayer was the soul of His Messianic ministry and Paschal Death."[81]

The Liturgy of the Hours is to be prayed in this spirit by us. Each Hour should be a key moment that embraces the ongoing reality comprising the whole of life. It should be a radiant moment in which a lived reality that sustains our being finds expression in a visible communal form.

If carried out in this spirit, the Liturgy of the Hours will enable us *to see Christ in all things*—in every event and action of our lives. These are signs that hold Him and when we pierce them we encounter Him. We are "strengthened to bring the Good News of Christ to those outside."[82] Each Hour becomes a new impetus to apostolic activity.

The Liturgy leaves its stamp on the whole of our life while our life in turn gives scope to the celebration of the Office. It enables us to overcome the fragmentation of our life by giving everything a *unity*, the one thing necessary. In everything we do, we are living for God at each moment.

The Liturgy of the Hours fosters our encounter with Christ and links our lives with His. By its relation with various times of our day, it accomplishes this purpose through a kind of "osmotic action" that pervades the day with prayer.

Through the saving power of the Eucharist, of which it is an extension (as we have indicated), the Office makes us ever more perfectly love Christ—if only we let it. It makes us "living sacraments" of Him. In the words of St. Ambrose:

> May the image [of Christ] shine forth in our profession of faith, in our love, and in our words and actions, so that His whole likeness may be mirrored in us, if possible. May He be our Head because "Christ is our Head." May He be our eye so that through Him we may see the Father. May He be our voice with which we speak to the Father. And may He be the hand with which we offer the sacrifice of our lives to God the Father.[83]

## The Liturgy of the Hours and the Laity

One of the most innovative features of the Liturgy of the Hours is its accent on the role of the laity in it. "Like the other Liturgical Actions, the Liturgy of the Hours is not something private but something that belongs to the whole Body of the Church, which it manifests and influences. . . . When the Liturgy of the Hours is celebrated . . . the people should take part in it as far as possible."[84]

This is an ideal that is difficult to realize. Yet it can be done—perhaps not with the whole parish community or even a large part of it but with small groups. For example, the Liturgy Committee or the Parish Council could take an active part in Evening Prayer from time to time.

In one case, a truncated form of Evening Prayer was used before every meeting of a Liturgy Committee and the members (twenty or so) liked it and became quite at home with it. They saw the prayer of the Church in action and they were able to use both words and silences to good effect.

The Liturgy of the Hours has its own ritual structure just as the Liturgy of the Eucharist does. It entails a proper setting or environment. The selection of place, furnishings (vestments, candles, participation materials, and so on), and their manner of use are important considerations. The seating arrangement for the participants should foster the sense of community, make the one who presides visible to all, and facilitate the common prayer of all.

The Bishops' Committee on the Liturgy[85] offers the following checklist: (1) chair for the one who presides; (2) ambo for the reader(s) and psalmist(s); (3) music stand for the director of song (if necessary); (4) candles; (5) flowers or plants; (6) chairs for acolytes; (7) participation books or materials; (8) incense, censer; (9) processional cross; (10) vestments (priest: alb, stole—cope is optional; deacon: alb, stole—cope is optional; cantor: alb—optional; acolyte: alb—optional).

Posture is also very important for participation.[86] All *stand* for: (1) introductory verses; (2) opening hymns; (3) Gospel Canticles; (4) prayers of intercession; (5) Lord's Prayer; (6) concluding prayer; (7) Blessing and Dismissal.

All *sit* for: (1) Psalms; (2) Psalm-prayers; (3) Canticles (except three noted above); (4) Antiphons: (5) Readings and Responses. All make the *Sign of the Cross* at: (1) the beginning of each Hour; (2) the beginning of the Gospel Canticles.

The entire celebration of the Liturgy of the Hours must be prepared to

## The Liturgy of the Hours: The Sanctification of Time

foster the prayer of the community. Good Liturgical Celebrations are those which are carried out with *dignity, attention, and devotion*. This is in turn the result of a deep faith that knows what is taking place and enlists heart, mind and voice in that sacred action.

The laity must be made to realize that the Liturgy of the Hours has the same relationship to their lives that the Eucharist does. It enables them to pray with the sentiments willed by God and the Church, and to identify with the actions of Christ, who by His life and self-offering gave glory to the Father and sanctified the life of all humankind.

Chapter 17
# LITURGICAL AND NON-LITURGICAL PRAYER: PRAYING WITH THE CHURCH

One definition of prayer is: "The attitude of heart that under the inspiration of the Holy Spirit opens itself to the Mystery of the Blessed Trinity."[87] Prayer is our response to God's Self-revelation made to us in Christ and transmitted to us through the Church in the Liturgy, the Bible, and daily Christian living.

In prayer we carry out in an eminent manner the priestly function of Jesus Christ, taking over in our hearts the very sentiments of the Total Christ—that is, Head and members. A prayer that rises from the depths of a silent heart fully inserted in the fiber of the Church, and fully attuned to her least vibrations, is by its nature an ecclesial prayer.

Prayer is a *response* to the God who has come—in Jesus Christ—to us. The initiative always comes from God and calls for our "obedience of faith," by which we put ourselves freely and completely in God's hands.[88]

There is evidence that many people nowadays pray less than they used to or at least that they pray with less faith. One of the reasons is that they recognize in their hearts a divided allegiance—to God and to the world. They give themselves over to their busy activities for the betterment of humankind and feel guilty for their lack of formal prayer.

This guilt stems from a narrow concept of prayer which looks upon prayer as exclusively words, thoughts, and desires addressed to God, a Someone in the beyond, a third entity besides the world and ourselves. The major reason for this is that popular teaching has so overstressed the transcendence of God as almost to neglect His immanence.

Yet Christ (and therefore God) penetrates the whole universe, the whole course of history, and humankind in particular. He enlightens every person whether that person knows it or not, and He pervades every part of the cosmos by His dynamic immanence.

Ultimately, prayer is nothing more than an encounter with this Person. Hence, meeting and serving others and also reflecting on and exploring life itself can be called prayer. For in such activities we encounter God, though often incognito, in His immanence.

Our every action (no matter how small or how secular) enables us to be in touch with God. It is God and God alone that devoted Christians pursue through the reality of created things. Our interest lies truly *in* things—but in absolute dependence upon God's presence in them.

The reason we can see God in the world is prayer—excentration of self in God. We refer our lives to another greater than ourselves. And the best way we do so is first by being what we are, then by loving, and finally by worship.

### Dialogue with God

Prayer means that we have extracted for ourselves the orthodox figure of a truly divine, omni-active Christ in whom we are conscious of living with complete joy and freedom, as in the sole real atmosphere of this world. It is the Church which guarantees us a response from this Divinity. She does so through her liturgical and sacramental life and her accent on prayer, both personal and liturgical.

To pray is to believe that God is a Person, Someone who listens and who replies and loves us. Prayer is the acceptance of being loved by God. Acceptance entails listening and responding, living a dialogue that should normally increase love.

Prayer thus means to live the Covenant of God with human beings, to enter into the revelation of Himself made by God the Father in the Holy Spirit to the human race through His creation, His chosen people, and ultimately through His Son Jesus. In this revelation, God speaks, and human beings speak, and God responds.

The Word became flesh and pitched His tent among us. He is, as we have seen, the sacrament of the encounter with God, the Great Sign.

Since He is God, Jesus is the Word of God addressed to humans. Since He is also Man, He is the Response of humans directed to God, the great *Yes* to God, the great *Prayer* to Him—throughout His whole life, on Calvary, and in His risen Presence on the altar.

Our great personal and communitarian prayer is the Mass—the Eucharistic Celebration where Christ calls us and awaits us so that He can pray in our midst! "He is able now and always to save those who approach God through Him because He is ever living to intercede for them. Such is the High Priest whom it was fitting for us to have—one who is holy, innocent, undefiled, separated from sinners, and made higher than the heavens" (Heb 7:25-26).

Each of the sacraments is thus *both an encounter and a prayer*: an encounter with Christ whose hand touches us through the medium of the Church's rite and an encounter with the Father in a particularly effective prayer: through Jesus Christ, His Son, our Lord, that we may be adopted, reconciled, confirmed, healed, united together in his love, and filled with the Holy Spirit.

The Spirit comes to us in power, light, and love, and inspires *prayer* and *adoration*, the adoration of Christ the Son Who cries out toward God: "Father." He enables us to pray in Christ, for we are "other Christs." He helps us to utter Christ's prayer: "Father."

Thus, prayer cannot be restricted to sacramental rites or receptions. Just as the sacraments must be lived so that their effects will perdure, so must prayer fill our lives. Prayer is an intervention of God in human space and time and the intervention (so to speak) of human beings in God's space and time.

The Sacraments introduce us into *Christian prayer*. Not the prayer of pagans or Mohammedans to the Most High God, all-powerful Creator and Sovereign Master of all things, but the prayer of Christ, of the Son to His beloved Father in the Spirit.

This prayer is also the prayer to Christ, our brother, and to Mary His mother, who is also our mother and the mother of the world. Finally, it is the prayer to our brothers and sisters in Christ—the Saints.

## Prayer—The Application of Christ's Redemption to "My World"

It is the power of prayer that keeps us close to Christ and that builds up the Body of Christ. True, the ultimate power comes from the Eucharist, as we have seen, but all other forms of prayer stem from it—recollection, mental prayer, purity of conscience, purity of intention, vocal prayer, or the sacraments.

These must be utilized to spread the efficacy of the Eucharist in any given situation, time, or place. Just as the Eucharist is the application of Christ's Redemption to the world as a whole, so my prayer flowing from the

Eucharist is an application of Christ's Redemption to *my entire world*, transforming it more and more into Christ.

Prayer is never carried out in isolation. It is always performed in contact with the real and in concert with the prayers and aspirations of the whole Mystical Body of Christ. Neither is prayer just a set of words but an attitude that spills over *into action*. It leads us closer to Christ and to fellow human beings.

In the Old Testament, we see the Psalms directing prayer toward the temporal and spiritual salvation of Israel. In the New Testament, we see the stress on the Incarnation of love in the heart of the real—especially in the Lord's Prayer which associates earth with heaven, the problems of human beings with the coming of God's Kingdom.

Thus, any prayer Christians make is always offered not in their own name or for themselves alone but in the name of and for the whole Body of Christ. Everything we do reflects on that Body either for good or for ill. Our prayer life is no different.

The Second Vatican Council took cognizance of this fact and called for a link between our personal prayer and liturgical prayer—the official prayer of the Body of Christ, so to speak. We should always pray in conjunction with the liturgical seasons and in the name of Jesus.

"The Liturgy is the summit toward which the activity of the Church is directed; at the same time, it is the fount from which all her power flows."[89] Accordingly, "prayers and devotions of the Christian people are to be so drawn up that they harmonize with the Liturgical Seasons, accord with the Sacred Liturgy, are in some fashion derived from it and lead the people to it."[90]

Christians are not content with merely adoring the beautiful harmonious presence of God in the universe. They inculcate in themselves utter receptivity to cooperate with the God who is operating at each moment in every event. Rather than running away from the world, they are totally at God's disposal to work in the world to bring it into greater spiritual existence, into greater unity of love—and find God in it.

Thus, it is in the actuality of our contemporary existence that praying must start. It comes forth from our concrete human situation for only *in this* can we have any real *relationship* with God.

Persons of prayer are those who habitually say Yes to God in any given situation, while resisting and even transferring the No which the same situation may contain. This response is one that comes from personal

## Liturgical and Non-Liturgical Prayer: Praying With the Church

freedom, a response given *from* the Spirit, the inner-dialogue partner, and from the love that He pours forth in our hearts.

For those who pray in this manner, Christ's presence impregnates and sustains all things. His power animates all energy. His life seeps into every other life and assimilates it to Himself. He makes everything in the world divinized, divinizing, and divinizable.

Every presence makes Christians feel that Christ is near. Every touch becomes the touch of His hand and every necessity transmits a pulsation of His will. Everything around us is transformed into the substance of His heart.

Christ effects a synthesis of all perfection and all growth in Himself. The act by which we unite with Him combines more attitudes than we could ever express. "Every affection, every desire, every possession, every light, every depth, every harmony, and every ardor glitters with equal brilliance, at one and the same time, in the inexpressible *relationship* that is set up between Christ and us!"[91]

### Devotions—Prayer in Action

Devotions may be looked at as a kind of "applied spirituality," a putting into practice of the particular spiritual way of life that we embrace. They are *prayer in action*. Hence, there are a multitude of different devotions in the Church—each suited to varying tastes of people.

The Church approves of devotions and encourages her people to make use of them. However, she insists that they be *in harmony with the Seasons of the Liturgy, accord with the Liturgy, and lead to the Liturgy*.

Over the years, some devotions that arose from the people (mostly in time of Liturgical decadence) became "pious exercises"—approved for recitation in public outside the Liturgy such as the Stations of the Cross or Benediction of the Blessed Sacrament.

Other devotions were even incorporated into the Liturgy itself, for example, much of the Service on Good Friday. This fact alone gives evidence of the Church's high regard for legitimate devotions.

Such devotions lead people to closer union with God, and impart a deeper spiritual life, either through their particular practice or through the persons invoked in them—Mary and the Saints (or even the Persons of the Trinity).

Non-liturgical devotions (which are non-liturgical prayer and actions) have much to offer Christians. For devotions have a totally different approach from the Liturgy and can appeal to other parts of the human makeup.

1) Devotions give us a chance to be the *subject* of the action and to express our *individual* needs. The Liturgy makes us the *object* of the action and gives us *edification*.

2) Devotions accentuate *persons*. The Liturgy concentrates on *themes*, for the most part. Thus, by the practice of devotions we are more closely associated with the Saints and other members of the Mystical Body.

3) Devotions are *centered on Christ*. The Liturgy is directed to the *Trinity*—it is addressed to the Father through the Son in the Holy Spirit. We can thereby obtain a *greater experience of closeness* to Christ through devotional practices.

4) Devotions are *simply structured* and possess a *simple theme*. The Liturgy is *highly formalized* and usually possesses a *multiplicity of themes*. Hence, devotions are easy to understand, easy to practice, and easy to identify with.

5) Devotions follow the *rhythm of prayer* and utilize the *language of prayer* exclusively. The Liturgy follows an elaborate *rhythm of instruction, logic, and prayer*. Devotions help us say what we mean and mean what we say.

6) Devotions are *colorful* in a way that people can understand. The Liturgy is *elevated* and sometimes appears *flat* and devoid of mystery. Thus, devotions can reflect our life situations and conditions more convincingly.

7) Devotions are usually *unvarying*. The Liturgy is *alive and changing*. Devotions are thus more reassuring in their *stability*, while the Liturgy presents something of a threat by its *changeability*.

Devotions can provide people with something that they may not find in the Liturgy too readily. That is their reason for existence.

Devotions should accord with the mind of the Church and are like extensions of the Liturgy (the Prayer of the Church) in our lives. Such devotions must be based on the fourfold principle set forth by Paul VI in his Apostolic Exhortation on Marian Devotion.

1) They should have a *biblical basis*, arising from the prayerbook par excellence. They should lead the people to listen to God's Word and respond to it by prayers and hymns which echo the words of Scripture.

2) They should have a *liturgical orientation*. As already mentioned,

*Liturgical and Non-Liturgical Prayer: Praying With the Church* 161

they should arise from the Liturgy and lead back to better Liturgical worship.

3) They should have an *ecumenical character*. As such they should be stripped of all exaggeration and incorrect practices that would hinder Christian unity. They must lead unerringly to Christ our Head and the source of unity with one another.

4) They must possess an *anthropological awareness*. They should not be linked with any particular living conditions but must manifest holiness as stemming from hearing God's Word, reflecting on it, and putting it into practice in a spirit of love and service. They must also be adapted to new perspectives that are uncovered by the human sciences.

Already new devotions are coming into wide acceptance, or rather old devotions are being adapted in accord with this fourfold principle and taking hold among the people.

We have seen the advent of the Scriptural Rosary with a greater emphasis on the words of Scripture for every Mystery. We have even seen the call of Paul VI to add to the Mysteries of the Rosary.

A very popular form of the Stations of the Cross in recent years is one based on the Scriptures more closely instead of the pious remarks of a Saint or writer. There is also the addition of a Fifteenth Station for the Resurrection, to bring this devotion into accord with the Church's accent on the Resurrection as the culmination of the Passion and the completion of the Paschal Mystery.

Finally, there are the many Bible Services that are commonly used in schools and in parishes, where the Word of God is honored, proclaimed, and gives life to the people in accord with the seasons of the year.

No matter what devotion is practiced, it can bring us closer to God by leading us to the Liturgy, the fount and apex of all Christian prayer.

### The Four Ends of Prayer

Traditionally, prayer is described as possessing a fourfold division, as having four purposes: (1) adoration, (2) praise and thanksgiving, (3) reparation or repentance, and (4) petition or supplication. This division is still useful for it gives the essential elements of the relation of human beings to God.

We *adore God* as the "Ground of our being," our Creator and Lord, on Whom we depend for our very existence. We give Him *thanks and praise* as our unending Benefactor and our gratuitous Redeemer. We beg Him *to forgive* our human failings and strengthen us as our unique Sanctifier. We ask His *help* in our daily existence as our loving Father in accord with the express word of Jesus.

These four ends are all based on *love for God* and in reality never occur all alone—they are invariably mingled with one or other of the ends. The division is merely an arbitrary one—to remind us of what we should pray for.

Prayer of petition is often looked down upon as the lowest type of prayer—the "gimme" prayer. As such, it has even fallen into some measure of disuse among the more thoughtful Christians. It is looked upon as too demanding and too close to the magical to be worth anything.

Yet in a very real way all prayer is essentially prayer of petition. Whether we thank God, worship or praise Him, or beg His forgiveness, our prayer is always one of "petition"—since we are *asking God for Himself*.

In the more *traditional way* of looking at things it is rather hard to see what prayer can do to change an all-knowing, all-foreseeing, and all-powerful God; at best it serves as a kind of experience of dependence before God. Secondly, we seem to be begging God to intervene in an abnormal way and change the arrangement of the cosmos.

But if we explain prayer in an *evolving* world, the action may be easier to understand. In such a world in which we cooperate with God to build up ourselves and everything around us into the fullness of the Body of Christ, petitionary prayer attains its real importance. It becomes a *sharing of our concerns* in collaboration with the creative work of God in the universe.

We freely contribute to the upbuilding of the universe by our acts, and God's concrete manner of caring for the universe will be influenced in some way by our creative choices. We do not ask God to come down and supernaturally transform reality according to our wishes. Rather we present our concerns regarding our own creative involvements so that they may enter into His constant shaping of the universe *in response to* the free and creative acts of creatures.

God offers possibilities, and human beings actualize them by acting (by prayer). The realities thus created are accepted and given permanent significance making them available for future creative acts. If we pray and cooperate with God, the world becomes friendly and good to us. We can literally change the world by our prayer *for it is in our power to "create" it*.

Thus, our prayer becomes very necessary. It is neither a luxury nor a sham. If we do not pray for such a thing, something will be forever missing even if such an eventuality does come about.

### Prayer in a Pluri-Providential World

This way of looking at prayer holds that we have received from our Savior the powers of mastering fortune so to speak. We can so control the chances of existence as to make them work in our favor. Scripture tells us that for those who love God and put that love in action, prayer and everything work together for their good (Rm 8:28).

Indeed, the global progress of things is in itself *one progress*. However, we must realize that it adds up to much more than one progress—a manifold one. It adds up to as many different aspects as there are conscious minds and to as many variable individually isolated aspects.

God's divine foreknowledge controls the progress of the whole as a function of the freedom of each one. Hence, it is as if there were, in the single event-system that determines the state of the universe at any given moment, as many *independent providences* as there are people in the world.

Thus, each of us has *our own universe*. We are at the center of such a universe and we are called to introduce harmony into it, just as though we were alone in the nature of things.

This may be termed a "polyvalence of the cosmos" which enables prayer to exercise a *creative* pre-action in the totality of phenomena. And it enables us to understand how each one of us, by confident prayer, can *change our own future* without impinging on that of our neighbor and without even disturbing the natural course of things in any scientifically verifiable way.

We live in two worlds at one time—the present reality and an eschatological reality, a world of interpersonal relationships. Through the Incarnation Christ entered into the *present world* and through the Resurrection He entered into the *eschatological* world. He thus brought them together so that we may live at once in both—through His grace and the power of the Spirit.

God works through chance and through the freedom of human beings by controlling the collective play of causes. Prayer enables us to enter into this creative power and see it at work all around us.

The importance of the events that develop us spiritually cannot be gauged by the rules or dimensions of the material order. The degree of creative energy in any event has nothing in common with the mechanical magnitude of that event.

From our vantage point all we see is disorder of chance events all around us. The future appears chaotic and questionable. But from God's vantage point, everything hangs together, everything makes sense, everything has its own purpose.

Once we accept the fact that the world is "pluri-providential," things begin to take on clarity and stability. We begin to discern better the "signs of the times" and to get into closer touch with the spiritual essential of life. We begin to pray in harmony with God's will for us and for the whole world.

We come to the realization that prayer has effects that we do not see—because they affect the totality of events that are influenced by faith or because God's adaptations of the visible universe to the requirements of our individual soul are done in view of success in heaven and not only a success on earth.

Even if we pray with all our strength, we learn that fortune will not necessarily come in the way we wish but in the way that is ordained for us. Petitionary prayer has two levels. The first is when we ask that we may be what we have to be in the circumstances confronting us—as we see things. The second level is when we are able to desire what God desires in any situation—as He sees things.

Ultimately, the latter is letting "God be God" in our lives—to a heroic degree. It is a prayer of complete trust in God, an acknowledgment that He knows what is good for us and, if we let him, He will indicate it to us.

We must accept God as our sole support in a true act of interior surrender. We must accept His Providence as being as physically real as the objects of our disquietude. In our suffering of the ills we have incurred, our remorse for the sins we have committed, and our vexation over the opportunities we have let slide by, we must pray without hesitation that God will turn each particular evil into good. Above all, we must *believe* it.

We are totally dependent on grace for peace and for the longing for God. In ourselves we can do nothing—but with God's help we can do a great deal. Yet we must realize that even with God's help we must contribute our part—otherwise again we will achieve nothing!

We are like an object illuminated by a searchlight. The object can neither force the searchlight's beam to begin to fall upon it nor make it continue to fall upon it. We can, however, pray for the light and be certain that it will never leave us.

*Liturgical and Non-Liturgical Prayer: Praying With the Church* 165

The most consoling part for us is that we can pray at all times no matter what we are doing. If we do our work with a view to building up the Body of Christ, we are always in tune with God, seeing Him everywhere and dialoguing with Him. We are praying as we live.

Chapter 18
# A LITURGICAL PERSON— A PERSON WHO LOVES LIFE

Christianity is Christ's Good News. It is a Mystery which contains the Incarnation (the invisible God's visible appearance in our midst), the act of Redemption on the Cross culminating in the Resurrection through which Jesus manifested His glory.

He did not show that glory to the whole world—only to the few witnesses whom God had chosen (Ac 10:40f), and through them to the Church. The Parousia (Christ's Second Coming in glory) will terminate this plan of salvation.

In the "Time between the times," the Church lives by faith and in the mysteries of Christ's worship. These mysteries are a working out and an explication of Christ's Paschal Mystery.

This working out is accomplished through *word* and *sacrament* or *rite*. Both aspects must be true. The Word must mean what it says and the Sacramental Act must mean what it signifies. Here is where modern persons must be made aware of the genuine meanings of *word* and *rite*, of Liturgy.

Modern persons find God a burden. The more science unveils the natural aspects of what were regarded as part of the mystery of God, the more a burden God becomes. The reason is that the God in question is no longer the God of our ancestors who has been handed down to us.

The God of our day must be thought of in terms that are a thousand times greater than the terms of the God of the past. The world as we know it is made up of staggering numbers, and human beings are much more complex than previously imagined. Hence, our God must be mind-boggling.

Under these circumstances, God loses His mystery, and so does nature. Nature is no longer a symbol, a transparency of higher realities.

It is *technology* which makes "miracles" in our day, and it is at our beck and call. It is the greatest of spiritual workers, providing us with instant service, information, and gratification. Why do we need a Divinity?

Even the *human person* has been stripped of all mystery. Depth psychology has explored the psyche and come up with all kinds of knowledge and methods of operation.

How then can contemporary people really appreciate word and rite in the Liturgy? Words couched out of past experience and rites developed out of past cultures?

The sole answer is for modern persons to be "Liturgical persons," to know, live, and love the Liturgy.

### A Technological Person

The first mark that persons of the Liturgy must have is to be a *real part* of their *life-situation*—something that liturgists have come to call "a *technological* person."

We should be faithful to our age. We do not live in the Middle Ages where faith overwhelmed life, so to speak, nor in the early days of the Church with its wide-scale persecution and wholesale martyrdom. We live, for the most part, in what is termed post-Christian civilization—a desacralized civilization.

Thus, what we feel about life is different from what Christians of other ages felt. But we have the same ultimate goal—union with God.

Yet we attain this goal in a different fashion. We *emphasize* our human condition.

> The laity need the kind of fraternal charity which will lead them to share in the living conditions, labors, sorrows, and hopes of their fellow human beings, and which will gradually dispose the hearts of all around them for the saving work of grace. They need a full awareness of their role in building up society, an awareness which will keep them preoccupied with bringing Christian largeheartedness to the fulfillment of their duties whether family, social, or professional.[92]

This means that we bring a different mentality to the Liturgy. Accordingly, we must bring our experiences, conditions, joys, and hopes there and combine them with the wealth of spirituality found therein. In so doing, we will create for ourselves a *Liturgical* spirituality. The Liturgy will take *our experiences* and transform them into means of growing in Christ. It will help us to build a world for Christ, a world ready for His Second Coming.

Many people shrink from such a thing. How can they possibly do this, they ask. They are not *clerics*, nor even *religious* persons! They can do it however, *because* Christ has empowered them to do so. Through the Liturgy, we can "Christify" the world simply by doing our ordinary tasks of life. The Liturgy will enable us to do this—if only we remain faithful to our part, bringing our world to the Liturgy as it is, with our problems, joys, hopes and fears.

## A Biblical Person

Besides *being ourselves*, we must also bring to the Liturgy an *interest in Biblical* things. We must be willing to learn the characteristics of the Bible. Many of them are shown in the Bible Readings in the Liturgy. But we must strive to read them beforehand in order to really integrate them in our Liturgy.

This means we must have the following attitudes:

1) We must accept the fact that God speaks to us in *words and actions*. Every event, every encounter, every conversation can be carrying a message from God—if we train our eyes to *see it*.

2) We must accept the fact that we are part of a *living History of Salvation*. Thus, we not only experience the History of Salvation, we also collaborate in it—we "make" it.

3) We must realize that God wants to be *part of our lives*. He has a plan for each of us—one that is unique and unrepeatable. It gives us a dignity and a value that are incalculable.

4) We must realize that God is with us in everything we do, that we live in the *Divine Milieu*. We are never far from God.

## A Poetic Person

We must also be poetic. This means taking a respite from the cares of the world—looking at the deeper side of life, doing something for no reason from time to time.

It means *seeing* something that is not apparent, *hearing* something that is drowned out by the hurly-burly of life, *saying* something that is not possible, *doing* something that is not programmed.

It means being willing to accept signs, symbols, and substitutes in place of the Real Thing, for the Real Thing is greater than anything available to us.

In short, it means *seeing God everywhere* under one of His many disguises—the poor, the lowly, the sick, the disadvantaged—but also in the rich who are confused, the influential who are weak, and the advantaged who are lost.

### A Fully Human Person

It becomes clear, then, that the persons of the Liturgy are those who are *fully human*. They enter fully into human living and they thus become fully Christian and fully worshipful.

> Modern humankind is on the road to a more *thorough development of its own personality, and to a growing discovery and vindication of its rights*. The Church has been entrusted with the task of revealing the Mystery of God, Who is the ultimate goal of human beings. Accordingly, she opens up to them at the same time the meaning of their own existence, that is, the innermost truth about themselves.... Whoever follows after Christ, the perfect Man, becomes more human.[93]

At the Last Supper, Christ prayed not that the Father would take His followers out of the world but that He would guard them in the world—to consecrate them in truth (Jn 17:15-18). In other words, He asked that they might be what they were intended to be by the Father—true human beings living up to the Divine image in them.

To be closer to God is to be more truly human. Moreover, the more human we are, the more "poetic" we will be and the more Biblical, and the more technological. All we need is the *will* to enter into this new field.

Many "ordinary" Christians are already in this field—without knowing it. They are truly living their human lives and their Christian lives—but they are doing so in *separate* compartments.

What they must do is bring these two areas together. And they can do so simply by being aware that these compartments are fully compatible. The human gives rise to the Christian and the Christian gives rise to the human.

It is up to us to develop all our human capabilities—not for themselves so much as for their use in God's service. There is an old theological axiom that *grace builds on nature*. The more developed is nature (or the human), the more effective will be the grace we receive.

Liturgical persons take care to develop their human potentialities to the fullest. They integrate their whole unique personalities into the service of God. They become not just Christians but Christians of a particular inalienable stamp. They become the Christian that God wants each to be—with the special nuances that He gave each one to develop, explore, and fulfill for His glory and their individual salvation.

## An Ecclesial Person

The Church is essentially our link with Christ and God. Without the Church, the power of the Incarnation would terminate. Hence, we must *cling to the Church*. We must be *persons of the Church*.

It is the specific function of the Church to Christianize all that is human. The energy for this process of Christification is *grace*, the energy of Christ, found in the sacraments, especially the Eucharist. This is the chief bond of union between the Incarnate Word and human beings (and ultimately all creatures).

The Church is indeed a "supernatural" organism—but in such a way that she is part and parcel of ordinary life. The Church is not extraneous to the lives of people. She is a most essential part of their lives.

The Church enables the world to go on and human beings to take their rightful place in it. She does this by uplifting and encouraging, by bringing Christ to people.

She is a bulwark of strength and hope, transforming the world through the Eucharist and showing how to turn sadness into joy. It is not a Church that knows all the answers, but it is a Church that constantly seeks for answers.

To be a liturgical person means to be *in tune with the Church*, to love the Church, to realize that she is a gift of God to us, a true Mother.

> She is humble and majestic. She professes to integrate every culture and to sum up in herself every value, and she desires at the same time to be the home of the little, the poor, the simple, and forlorn multitude. She does not cease for an instant . . . to contemplate Him Who is at once the Crucified One and the Risen One, the Man of Sorrows and the Lord of Glory—He Who was conquered by the world and Who is the Savior of the world.[94]

To the Church go our common love, our thoughts, and our service, for she is the living picture of God's love for us, the *Sacrament of salvation*. Above all, we must bring all of ourselves to her because she is our Mother.

"To have God as our Father, we must first have the Church as our Mother."[95] Hence, we must "*love* this Church, *be in* this Church, and *be* this Church."[96]

## A "Christ" Person

The Church is our Mother; she is the presence of the Triune God in our world. She is a community of divine love in the world. She makes us "other Christs" and gives us a share in Christ's threefold office of Priest, Prophet, and King. And by sharing that office in our lives we become true Liturgical Persons.

The *priestly office* of Christ enables us to offer spiritual worship for the glory of God and the salvation of human beings. We have been given the Holy Spirit, called, and wonderfully prepared for this. All we need to do is *tune in to* the Spirit.

Thus, all our works, prayers, and apostolic endeavors as well as our family lives, our daily occupations, our physical and mental relaxation, and even our hardships in life all can become "spiritual sacrifices acceptable to God through Jesus Christ" (1 P 2:5).

Together with the offering of the Lord's Body, these are most fittingly offered by us in the celebration of the Eucharist. We thus really *consecrate* the *world itself* to God.

Christ, the great Prophet, proclaimed the Kingdom of His Father both by the testimony of His life and by the power of His words. He now continually fulfills His prophetic office until the complete manifestation of His glory. He does this through all Christians, so that the power of the Gospel might shine forth in daily and family life.

We are to conduct ourselves as children of the promise. Thus, strong in faith and hope, we make the most of the present, and with patience await the glory that is to come.

We do this (1) by announcing Christ through a living testimony as well as through the spoken word in the ordinary surroundings of the world: (2) by a supernatural sense of faith which joins all other members of the Church in expressing its consent in matters of faith and morals; and (3) by the special graces (charisms) that render each person suitable to take

## A Liturgical Person—A Person Who Loves Life

charge of diverse works and functions useful for the renewal and development of the Church (cf. 1 Cor 12:7).

The Risen Christ entered into the glory of the Kingdom. To Him all things are made subject until He subjects Himself and all created things to the Father so that God may be all in all. Christ has communicated this *kingly* power to His followers so that they may be constituted in royal freedom and by true penance and holy life may conquer the reign of sin in themselves.

Thus, we are called to serve Christ in our fellow human beings so that we may by humility and patience lead them to the King.

We must learn the deepest meaning and value of all creation as well as its role in the harmonious praise of God. We must assist one another to live holier lives in our daily occupations. In this way, the world may be permeated by the spirit of Christ and it may more effectively fulfill its purposes in justice, charity, and peace. All we need to do is open our hearts and minds and cooperate with the Grace God gives us. He will do the rest.

He will give our lives a dimension that they never had before, a dimension that helps us live them to the full, and a dimension that gives us a foretaste of heaven on earth.

# FOOTNOTES

1. Vatican II: *Constitution on the Sacred Liturgy*, no. 14.
2. *Ibid.*
3. *Ibid.*, no. 48.
4. Homily at Phoenix Park, Dublin, September 29, 1979.
5. Robert Hovda, "It Begins with the Assembly" in *The Environment for Worship* (Washington, D.C.: USCC Publications, 1980), p. 37.
6. Vatican II: *Constitution on the Sacred Liturgy*, no. 14.
7. General Instruction to the Roman Missal, no. 58.
8. *The Becoming of the Church* (New York: Paulist Press, 1974), p. 45. See also R. Wayne Kraft, *Symbols, Systems, Science and Survival* (New York: Vantage Press, 1975), pp. 1-3.
9. See Jerry Hill, *Ian Ramsey: To Speak Responsibly of God* (London: George Allen & Unwin Ltd., 1976), pp. 17-32.
10. Dane Archer and Robert Akent, "How Well Do You Read Body Language?" *American Science Annual*, 79 (Grolier Inc. 1978), pp. 42-49.
11. Gustave Martelet, *The Risen Christ and the Eucharistic World* (New York: The Seabury Press, 1976), p. 43.
12. "Religion and Science: A Philosopher's Approach" in *Church Quarterly Review* (January-March 1961), pp. 77ff.
13. Avery Dulles, *Models of the Church* (New York: Doubleday & Co., 1974), p. 18.
14. Vatican II: *Dogmatic Constitution on Divine Revelation*, no. 12.
15. Pius XII, *Divino Afflante Spiritu*, nos. 33-34; Vatican II, *Dogmatic Constitution on Divine Revelation*, nos. 11-12.
16. *Constitution on the Sacred Liturgy*, no. 7.
17. Prologue to *Order of Readings for Mass*, Second Typical Edition 1981, reproduced in *Notitiae*, pp. 180-183 (July-October 1981), no. 10, p. 366.
18. *Ibid.*, no. 3, p. 362.
19. See, for example, U.S. Bishops' Commission on the Liturgical Apostolate, "The Use of Vernacular at Mass," October 29, 1964.
20. Prologue to *Order of Readings for Mass*, *loc. cit.*, no 4, p. 363.
21. *Ibid.*, no. 6, p. 364.
22. *Constitution on the Sacred Liturgy*, no. 47.
23. *Ibid.*, no. 11.
24. *Ibid.*, no. 48.
25. Vatican II: *Constitution on Divine Revelation*, no 21.
26. General Instruction of the Roman Missal, no. 68.
27. *Constitution on the Sacred Liturgy*, no 28.
28. *Ibid.*, no. 33.
29. Pius XII, *Mediator Dei*, no. 20.
30. No. 7.
31. No. 39.
32. Paul VI, *Apostolic Exhortation on the Renewal of Religious Life*.
33. Allocution of December 10, 1973.
34. *Instruction on the Eucharistic Mystery*, no. 38.

35. Joseph Gelineau, "The Nature and Role of Signs in the Economy of the Covenant" in *Worship* 39 (November 1965), p. 530.
36. *Ibid.*, p. 531.
37. *Ibid.*, pp. 531-532.
38. See *Constitution on the Church in the Modern World*, no. 11.
39. Gelineau, *art. cit.*, p. 538.
40. Angelus Haussling in Karl Rahner (ed.), *Encyclopedia of Theology* (New York: The Seabury Press, 1975), art. "Liturgy," p. 865.
41. Encyclical *Quas Primas: On the Kingship of Christ*.
42. *Constitution on the Sacred Liturgy*, no. 33.
43. *Third Instruction on the Implementation of the Constitution on the Sacred Liturgy*, no. 13.
44. Letter to All Bishops (February 24, 1980): *The Lord's Supper*, I, no. 6.
45. "Work, Leisure, and Contemplation" in *Spiritual Life*, vol. 16, no. 4 (Winter 1970), p. 189.
46. Cyprian Vagaggini, *Theological Dimensions of the Liturgy* (Collegeville, Minn.: The Liturgical Press, 1976). pp. 191f.
47. For many of the points made in this section, I am indebted to articles that are found in *Ephemerides Liturgicae* 90 (1976), nos. 3-6.
48. *Against Heresies*, 4, 20, 7.
49. *Signum Magnum*, May 13, 1967.
50. The full text may be found in the May-June 1981 issue of *Notitiae* (pp. 247-267) together with an excellent commentary by Ignazio M. Calabuig, O.S.M. ("Significato e Valore del Nuovo 'Ordo Coronandi Beatae Mariae Virginis' "—"Significance and Value of the New 'Rite for Crowning the Blessed Virgin Mary' ": pp. 268-324) which forms the basis for the following thoughts.
51. *Constitition on the Church*, no. 59.
52. Paul VI: *Devotion to the Blessed Virgin Mary*, no. 6.
53. *La Evangelización en el Presente y en el Futuro de America Latina* (Evangelization in the Present and in the Future of Latin America) (Mexico: Ediciones CEM, 1979), pp. 101, 103, 132.
54. Pius XII: *The Queenship of Mary*.
55. *Constitution on the Church*, no. 53.
56. Numbers 36-37.
57. *Constitution on the Sacred Liturgy*, no. 103.
58. *Constitution on the Church*, nos. 59, 61.
59. *Against Julian*, 1, 5, 21.
60. Vatican II: *Constitution on the Church*, no. 40.
61. *Encyclical on the Sacred Liturgy (Mediator Dei)*, no. 167.
62. Vatican II: *Constitution on the Church*, no. 42.
63. Vatican II: *ibid*.
64. *Constitution on the Church in the Modern World*, no. 38.
65. *Ibid.*, no. 40.
66. *Ibid.*, no. 41.
67. Vatican II: *Constitution on the Church*, no. 48.
68. *Ibid.*, no. 1.
69. *General Introduction of the Liturgy of the Hours*, no. 12.
70. *Ibid*.
71. *Ibid.*, no. 194.
72. Odo Casel, *The Mystery of Christian Worship and Other Writings* (Westminster, Md.: The Newman Press, 1963). p. 89.
73. *General Introduction of the Liturgy of the Hours*, no. 13.
74. *Constitution on the Sacred Liturgy*, no. 83.
75. *Discourse on Psalm 85, 1.*
76. *General Introduction of the Liturgy of the Hours*, no. 20.
77. *Ibid.*, no. 56.
78. *Ibid.*, no. 140.
79. *Ibid.*, no. 55.

80. *Ibid.*, no. 169.
81. *Ibid.*, no. 4.
82. *Ibid.*, no. 18.
83. *Concerning Isaac and the Soul*, 8, 75.
84. *General Introduction of the Liturgy of the Hours*, no. 20.
85. *The Liturgy of the Hours: Study Text VII* (Washington, D.C.: USCC, 1981), p. 36.
86. *Ibid.*, p. 37.
87. Boniface Baroffio, *Liturgia e Preghiera* (Turin: Marietti, 1981), p. 45.
88. Vatican II: *Constitution on Divine Revelation* no. 5.
89. *Constitution on the Sacred Liturgy*, no. 10.
90. *Ibid.*, no. 13.
91. Teilhard de Chardin, "The Mystical Milieu" in *Writings in Time of War* (New York: Harper and Row, 1967), p. 147.
92. Vatican II: *Decree on the Apostolate of the Laity*, no. 13.
93. Vatican II: *Constitution on the Church in the Modern World*, no. 38.
94. Henri de Lubac, *Meditazione sulla Chiesa* (Brescia, 1967), p. 327.
95. St. Cyprian, *On the Unity of the Church*, ch. 6.
96. St. Augustine, *Sermon 138*.